The Gardener's Guide
to Growing
FRITILLARIES

The Gardener's Guide to Growing
FRITILLARIES

Michael Jefferson-Brown
Kevin Pratt

DAVID & CHARLES
Newton Abbot

TIMBER PRESS
Portland, Oregon

PICTURE ACKNOWLEDGEMENTS

Alpine Garden Society 50, 54–5, 65, 71; Karl Adamson 12, 18, 23, 25, 32, 36, 47, 51, 74, 77; Francis Ferns 41, 42, 53, 80, 113; Michael Jefferson-Brown 6, 40, 67; Kevin Pratt 39, 44–5, 66, 113; Justyn Willsmore 1, 2, 3, 8, 10, 11, 13, 15, 17, 22, 26, 27, 28, 29, 30, 31, 34, 38, 43, 48, 49, 52, 54, 56, 57, 58–9, 60, 63, 64, 68, 70, 75, 78, 82, 83, 85, 86, 87, 88, 91, 92, 93, 95, 96, 97, 100–1, 102, 103, 104-5, 108, 109, 111, 115, 116, 117, 118, 119, 122, 123, 124–5, 127, 130, 131, 132, 134, 136, 137

Illustrations on pages 14, 16 and 20 by Coral Mula

NOTE Throughout the book the time of year is given as a season to make the reference applicable to readers all over the world. In the northern hemisphere the seasons may be translated into months as follows:

Early winter	December	*Early spring*	March	*Early summer*	June	*Early autumn*	September
Midwinter	January	*Mid-spring*	April	*Midsummer*	July	*Mid-autumn*	October
Late winter	February	*Late spring*	May	*Late summer*	August	*Late autumn*	November

First published in the UK in 1997 by David & Charles Publishers,
Brunel House, Newton Abbot, Devon
ISBN 0 7153 0229 9

First published in North America in 1997 by Timber Press Inc.,
133 SW Second Avenue, Suite 450, Portland, Oregon 97204, USA
ISBN 0-88192-387-7
Cataloguing-in-Publication Data is on file with the Library of Congress

Typeset by ACE
and printed in Italy by Lego SpA

Photographs page 1 *F. aurea*; page 2 *F. hermonis amana*; page 3 *F. bucharica*

CONTENTS

INTRODUCTION

The fritillaries are a genus of around 100 species. These are spread over a wide area of the temperate parts of the Northern Hemisphere, with a single species native to Britain and a cluster at home around the Balkans and in Asia Minor. They are bulbous plants allied to the lily complex of the *Lilium*, *Nomocharis* and *Notholirion* genera and are also related to tulips, although not quite as closely.

This is an exciting genus which deserves the kind of dedication that hellebores inspire from gardeners. They are plants that require some knowledge and care, but a fine collection could be housed in a small area – only a fraction of that needed for a similarly comprehensive gathering of hellebores. They have all the prerequisites for a huge surge in popularity, being beautiful and varied, though their attractions are not those of dahlia-type showiness; they have more subtle charms, with often unusual colouring and distinctive flower forms and habits of growth.

The fascination these plants exert on their admirers could be extremely frustrating if they were all rare and inaccessible. Currently, though, *The RHS Plant Finder* lists well over 100 forms on sale. Of these, a good number can be planted in the expectation that they will thrive with minimal attention so that a newcomer's enthusiasm is not immediately dampened by disappointing results; while they look as exotic as orchids they are not necessarily difficult to cultivate. There are, however, many intriguing species needing more specialized culture which will provide a greater challenge for the more experienced gardener.

Many of the less common species are being grown by an expanding number of aficionados, some members of the flourishing Alpine Garden Society and others

of the popular Lily Group of the Royal Horticultural Society. There is a reservoir of expertise to tap into and one soon learns of the availability of many 'rare' kinds – much wider than might be thought at first.

Among the pots of the dedicated fritillary grower will be some rarer kinds and perhaps some labels indicating newly collected seed from Asia Minor or elsewhere bearing the exciting message 'species nova?' There is certainly still the possibility of new species being found in horticulturally remote corners of the world.

Apart from their visual attractions, fritillaries have another appeal – they are bulbous. Bulbs seem to have a special lure for gardeners, with their rapid growth and blooming and their capacity to increase dramatically in both size and numbers beneath the soil; it is so satisfying to plant one and raise many. It is not primarily the profit motive that causes pleasure, more the obvious wellbeing of the plants and the chance their propagation offers to swop plants with other specialists in the genus.

We have written this volume, the first for over 50 years devoted to fritillaries, to help to fill a gap in readily available information on the genus. Our advice is based on our experience, but we are all too aware that, as in all things horticultural, to lay down absolute rules is to invite ridicule; what may serve one garden may be very much less successful next door. The title, *The Gardener's Guide to Growing Fritillaries*, is an indication of the practical intent of the book. To review the scope of the genus and to give some indication of the interrelationships within it is an important part of it, but our main purpose has been to give guidance on cultivation – and to fire new enthusiasm for a set of plants that, once embarked upon, will prove addictive.

F. michailovskyi, a plant to be found in many garden centres.

1

THE FASCINATION
OF FRITILLARIES

Few bulbous genera can approach the variety of the fritillaries, for in size, form and habit they are extremely diverse. Such a wide-ranging genus would be merely an interesting academic study if they were not also possessed of beauty. They are both lovely and unusual, a combination that many gardeners find irresistible.

All species of fritillaries have charms of their own. A few – such as the crown imperials, which have been grown in gardens for centuries – are big, bold and brightly coloured, but the majority of species have more introvert appeal, their flowers normally painted in a range of unusual colourings. Some, such as *F. camschatcensis*, may be within a cat's whisker of pure black, and *F. persica* may be a rich purple-black enhanced to a lesser or greater degree by a lovely plum 'bloom'. More often the colourings are a mix of greens, pale yellows or mauves with areas of contrasting colours, perhaps with the petal tips a greeny-gold and the main bell a maroon purple as in *F. michailovskyi*, or maybe with one or more colours overlaid with a chequerboard patterning as, most noticeably, in the snake's head fritillary, *F. meleagris*, a type of colour patterning found in a number of *Nomocharis* but very rarely elsewhere. It is probably the flower colours that first attract newcomers to the *Fritillaria* genus. As the blooms are almost invariably an astonishing size for the stature of the plants, the unusual hues make a real impact.

A limited number of species were grown in our gardens through the nineteenth century, but during the twentieth the list has increased dramatically. Before the outbreak of World War II in 1939 a large number of species had been gathered in a relatively small number of gardens, but during the war and the difficult years immediately afterwards the numbers in cultivation dropped. It is in the past 50 years that the extent of the genus has begun to be recognized by discriminating gardeners as bulbs and seeds have been collected from the main areas where fritillaries grow wild. The Balkans and Asia Minor began to be more extensively explored after the war, and there may be new species still to be found there. Asian species that were found and introduced in the earlier part of the century are to some extent now being rediscovered, and many of the very interesting species from western North America, some of them under threat from land development, are becoming rather more available through bulb dealers and growers, though the rarer ones remain tricky to obtain.

There are at least 100 species worldwide, though some botanists would make many more by defining their species more closely. They range from only a few centimetres to 1m ($3^1/_4$ft) or so high, some with but a single flower, others with upwards of two dozen. Within a well-defined species there can be considerable variation of size, colour and habit. Gardeners may gain only a limited sense of the character of a species as a single specimen or identical members of a clone will suggest a uniformity of appearance completely contradicted by the species in the wild – though there are species that vary within very narrow limits. Also, botanists have not been free of the fault of prejudging the bounds of a species and taking a more restricted view than they would after seeing the plant in a variety of wild habitats. Synonyms abound. However, there is one point of

The snake's head fritillary, *F. meleagris* – a plant that is variable in colour but invariably attractive, with the bonus of easy cultivation.

F. *affinis* is probably the easiest of the American species to grow in the garden.

the country. Many species are easier than reputed and others are almost invariably difficult, though it is likely that clones or strains of more amenable plants may evolve within a tricky species. Accepting the challenge of cultivating some of the more rarely grown kinds with a detailed menu of likes and dislikes will be just what many plantspeople enjoy, while others will be satisfied with the easier species. Expert and novices will both be happy to enjoy the more trustworthy garden merits of such species as the following, which could be considered a 'starter collection': F. *acmopetala*, F. *affinis*, F. *camschatcensis*, F. *messanensis gracilis*, F. *imperialis*, F. *involucrata*, F. *latifolia*, F. *messanensis*, F. *meleagris*, F. *michailovskyi*, F. *montana*, F. *pallidiflora*, F. *pontica*, F. *pyrenaica*, F. *thunbergii*, F. *uva-vulpis*.

Aspiring collectors often want to grow their first precious bulbs in pots and there are many species, if not a

F. *messanensis gracilis*, a popular plant from northern Albania and Macedonia, is a neater, smaller form of F. *messanensis*, and may be very similar to it except that the central stripe and insides of the petals are yellower.

almost universal agreement and that is to take F. *meleagris* as the standard to which all may be compared.

Wild fritillaries are found at varying altitudes and in differing types of terrain. Some species are only found in specialized environments such as screes, meadows or woodland edges, while others are less demanding. A knowledge of their native habitats may prevent making major cultural errors, but often bulbs grow well in garden conditions very different to those in the wild; one may get much better results where they grow without hindrance and are not subject to climatic difficulties or the competition of surrounding vegetation and the depredations of goats, sheep and other livestock.

Attitudes to cultural methods vary considerably. What suits one garden in the driest part of East Anglia is not going to give as good results in the wettest part of

F. uva-vulpis is one of the most rapidly increasing plants in cultivation. It comes from eastern Turkey, Iraq and Iran, where it grows in moist spots up to 1,800m (6,000ft).

clear majority, that can be very good cultivated in this way. At the early flower shows where alpines are exhibited it is unusual not to see some *Fritillaria* species in pots. This may suggest to the onlooker that this is the way they must be grown, but this may not be the case; those that come into growth very early and may be damaged by repeated frosts are safer in a pot, but many species (more than previously realized) are perfectly happy grown in the open in suitable conditions. Groups of fritillaries flourishing in the open ground certainly create a more impressive picture than those same species in pots.

The increased enthusiasm for the genus is not difficult to understand as all the species look delightful,

they are unusual and they are well adapted to today's smaller gardens. A number are very widely available, while others are not too difficult to locate in the collections of commercial bulb and alpine specialists. The seed lists of specialist societies and of collectors widen the choice considerably, and the gardening fraternity that is dedicated to the *Fritillaria* genus seems to consist of very pleasant people who are more than happy to engage in friendly exchange or in giving away their surplus stock.

It would be wrong to give the impression that you can soon have a garden full of as much colour as dahlias and chrysanthemums can quickly provide. Nor is the normal cultural advice for bulbous genera applicable – in this case 'scratch a hole, throw in the bulb, cover and wait' is a little less than sufficient. Nevertheless, this genus is well worth the little extra effort that is required to produce a gratifying display.

F. biflora

F. camschatcensis

F. pontica

F. involucrata

F. aphrodite

F. acompetala
(dark form)

F. uva-vulpis

F. pallidiflora

F. pyrenaica

F. whittallii

PLATE I
All flowers are approximately ⅓ size

2

BOTANY & DISTRIBUTION

Fritillaries are members of the lily family, their nearest relatives being the genera *Lilium*, *Nomocharis* and *Notholirion*. The distribution of fritillaries is across the temperate part of the northern hemisphere rather in the same manner as the true lilies, though fritillaries spread into the drier, harsher areas of Asia Minor and California. There is a considerable correlation between the main areas of the worldwide distribution of the species and the botanical groupings within the *Fritillaria* genus; for example, the Liliorhiza section species are found only in North America, something one might expect to find but not always the case in other genera. For ease of access in this book the species are listed alphabetically rather than by geographical distribution or botanical affinities.

The aim of this chapter and the A–Z list is to give a clear idea of the botany of the plants without losing readers who are not familiar with the minutiae of botanical language. The varied forms of the fritillaries make their study interesting and no one should be daunted by what may seem at first glance a rather academic exercise. Some basic terms must be used and a glossary of these is given on page 138, but an instance of the reader-friendly approach to our study is the use in the text of the gardeners' inclusive term 'petal' in place of the more botanically correct 'tepal' for both outer sepal and inner petal of the flower.

FLOWERS

The majority of fritillary flowers are conspicuously large, though some, for example *F. brandegeei*, are of more modest proportions. Almost all species have pendant or semi-pendant flowers. The numbers carried on a stem range from a single one to over two dozen.

The distinctive *F. persica* may reach over 1m (3¹/₄ft) high and carry perhaps 30 flowers at a time.

The perianth is made of six tepals, the three outer sepals and the three inner petals, all six hereafter referred to as petals. The outer and inner petals are more or less the same size and colouring. If there are differences, the inner set are likely to be slightly narrower

STYLES

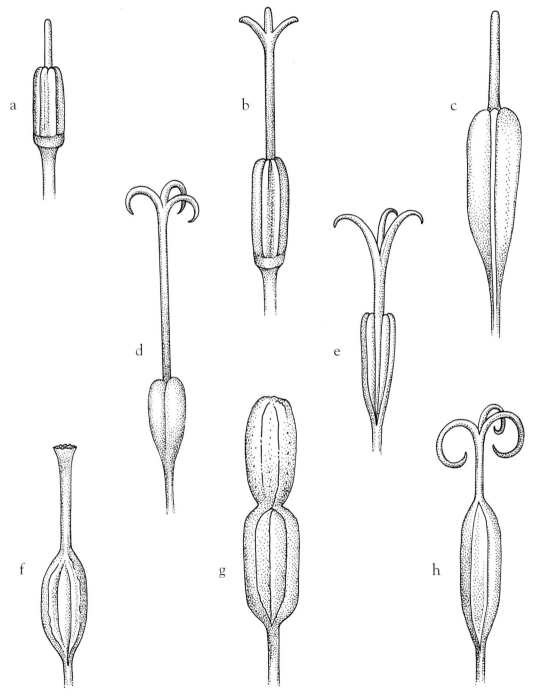

a, c, f, g = entire   b, d, e, h = trifid

and the outer three may have heavier colouring on the outer surfaces. Each inner petal has a well-developed nectary at its base, the shape of the nectary varying according to the species and serving as a diagnostic aid, although there can be some variation within a species.

Petal colouring may be fairly uniform within a species such as *F. thunbergii* or *F. persica*, but usually there is variation of colour and markings – sometimes surprisingly wide. As many species have two or more colours mixed in differing proportions and shades in different individuals, some more clearly marked than others, there is scope for bewilderment as well as admiration. Some species will have completely yellow or white forms.

Flower form is normally campanulate, with bells often wide-shouldered and almost as broad as deep, as in, for example, *F. meleagris* or *F. latifolia*. However, a good number have longer, more slender bells. The petal ends may be blunt and pointing downwards but many species, for example *F. recurva* or *F. michailovskyi*, have petal tips recurving outwards and curling backwards, in many *F. recurva* individuals the recurve more than completing the entire 360°. The cloche-hat of *F. meleagris* and others is exchanged for a wide coolie-hat style in species such as *F. micrantha* and the diminutive *F. brandegeei*, with flowers so open as to be almost starry. *F. karelinii* has widespread petals almost like a hellebore.

While orthodox flower pose is fully pendant, quite a number of species swing their bells some degrees towards the horizontal; in *F. brandegeei* and *F. camschatcensis* they are more or less completely horizontal.

Six anthers are held by filaments either by the base or towards their midpoint. They may be versatile (able to swing freely) or fixed. The style, while obvious, is shorter in proportion than that of most *Lilium* forms and does not protrude as much; it may end with an entire club-like stigma in the same form as most lilies, or may be divided into three and split into short or long arms – the trifid form. The style type is one of the most important diagnostic features, despite the fact that there can be some variation within a species.

The ovary contains three chambers with each having two rows of ovules, which, if fertilized, develop into flat disc-like seeds stacked one upon another like plates. Seed usually ripens to a brownish shade. The style falls away after becoming redundant in the same manner as in lilies. The fertilized ovaries swell and form ripe flat-topped capsules that split longitudinally in three to

F. michailovskyi, now known and favoured worldwide although it was only rediscovered two decades ago.

reveal and then to shed the six columns of seed. Fritillaria capsules vary in form: those of *F. imperialis* and *F. pallidiflora*, for example, are rather squat, squarish and somewhat wider than deep, while those of *F. involucrata* resemble many lily capsules in being rather longer than wide and gently tapered towards the base. *F. pontica* has longer pods, perhaps twice as long as wide.

BULB FORMS

The form of the bulb has long been regarded as one of the most important botanical features of the genus in trying to differentiate the species and evaluate their degrees of relationship. There is a good deal of variation in form, size and performance, and even within a species there can be a little variation in form and rather more in size. Often different strains or clones will have markedly different responses to such important matters as procreation and flower production.

Fritillary bulbs are usually made of only two thick scales, quite unlike those of lily bulbs; their texture is

BULB FORMS

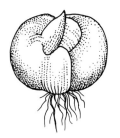

F. latifolia

F. liliacea

F. tubiformis

F. acmopetala

F. affinis

F. meleagris

F. pudica

F. camschatcensis

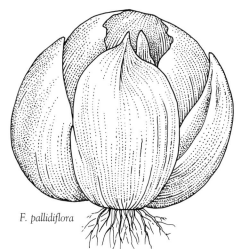

F. pallidiflora

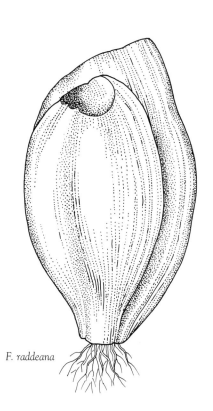

F. raddeana

F. *gibbosa*, a beautiful, distinct but none-too-easy species from Iran and Afghanistan.

much closer to that of tulip bulbs but if a tulip is cut open its scales will be found to be rounded and to have much smoother surfaces than those of fritillaries. Some species, such as F. *agrestis*, may have four or five thick scales joined at the base only. Others, for example F. *bucharica* and F. *gibbosa*, have a tunic around the bulb like a tulip, but much thinner. The previous season's flowering stem wastes away to leave a rounded cavity in the centre of the bulbs of most species.

American species have distinctive bulbs with, in some species, a series of much looser scales on their outer sides in the form of loosely attached 'rice grains', so called because of their size and shape. In the wild the grains can fall away from the parent bulbs and form new independent plants. The gardener carefully harvests these grains to increase stock, although they can take almost as long to reach flowering size as plants raised from seed. Grain-raised plants are of course genetically as one with the parent and all together represent a single clone, while plants raised from seed are genetically distinct individuals.

Bulbs range in size from the small ones about the size of a crocus species corm, and similarly flattened in form, to the large ones such as those belonging to F. *persica* and F. *imperialis*, which may be as big as a tennis ball.

LEAF & STEM FORMS

Fritillary stems are usually green but are sometimes coloured, may be polished or glaucous and are more or less upright with no branching. During their development the stems of some may start virtually horizontal and hoist themselves up day by day until at flowering time they are upright. The stems generally vary in height from a few centimetres to about 1m (3¼ ft), though some of the F. *imperialis* forms may reach 1–1.2m (3 ¼–4ft) high. The leaves may be produced at the base or not, while those on the stem may be scattered, alternate or whorled. Stronger individuals of a species may have some whorled leaves as well as scattered ones, while weaker bulbs have only scattered ones. The leaves may be highly polished, as in F. *imperialis*, but are often glaucous, as in F. *pyrenaica*. The leaf margins are entire without serration or divisions.

Leaf shapes vary from narrow grass-like foliage to wider forms with their broadest part towards the base (lanceolate), to the centre (oblanceolate) or somewhat more to the end (spatulate). The photograph on page 18 shows the various leaf forms.

CLASSIFICATION

To see *Fritillaria* species in the wild is to realize the extent of variation that is possible within the set limits of a species. Flower colour, the most obvious feature, can vary hugely within a species, but so can other features such as height, overall size, leaf form and overall performance. Individuals taken from the extremes of such specific variation have often been honoured with their own specific names and started a series of synonyms for what has later been seen to be one genetically governed species. Fritillaries have suffered from this syndrome more than most genera.

Modern techniques in genetic DNA 'fingerprinting' should make life easier in the future for those engaged in tidying up the nomenclature of the genus. There will always be different interpretations of the relationships of plants within the genus as this is a matter of approach, though some things are generally accepted as part of the received wisdom. However, at any one time the grid of names and group relationships imposed on the genus may slip one way or another as this is a dynamic group of plants that in evolutionary terms are relatively new and lively; their evolution has not always been accomplished in a neat uniform direction but more as a tortuous multidirectional spread influenced by chance and the vagaries of the environments in which they are found.

PLATE II
All leaves shown approximately ½ size

F. forbesii

F. camschatcensis

F. imperialis

F. affinis

F. biflora

The main features used to determine the specific status of fritillary species are: bulb form and size; style form; nectary size and form; flower form; flower colouring; leaf form; leaf colouring and texture; foliage arrangement. These features are of differing value within species and groups. The same features define the sections into which the genus is normally split, with the main diagnostic value being invested in bulb form.

SECTIONS OF THE GENUS FRITILLARIA

There have been several attempts at subdividing the genus in the past and we are following a conservative agenda in accepting six sections. These have evolved through the major work of Baker (1883), the updating work of Turill, the 1944 review of North American kinds by Dorothy Beetle, and latterly the important and continuing work of Martin Rix. We are maintaining the section Korolkowia with its solitary species *F. sewerzowii*. The Russian botanist Komarov (1935) suggested making this a separate genus, *Korolkowia*, and would have also given generic status to the Rhinopetalum.

The six *Fritillaria* sections are: 1) Eufritillaria; 2) Petilium; 3) Theresia; 4) Rhinopetalum; 5) Korolkowia; 6) Liliorhiza.

1 EUFRITILLARIA

This large section is in four main groupings, comprising species found growing in western Europe, the Mediterranean basin and western Asia. Their bulbs are normally composed of two scales and are often enclosed by the rudimentary beginnings of a tunic, the wasted tissue of previous years' scales. The flowers are normally borne singly, but there may be two to a stem or very occasionally three. The size and height of plants vary, as do the form, positioning and quantity of leaves. The styles may be split into three, an arrangement termed 'trifid', but can also be entire or three-lobed rather than divided. The differing styles have been made the basis of splitting this section into two subsections, Fritillaria for those with divided styles and Olyostyleae for the others (Martin Rix 1979). However we are following a newer grouping as shown in the table on page 21.

2 PETILIUM

Even a non-gardener would easily separate plants in this crown imperial group from the others as they are so much larger and sturdier. They grow wild in south-eastern Turkey, Turkestan, north-eastern Iraq, Iran and across to the western Himalayas. The bulbs are much larger than those of other sections except the Theresia with its solitary species. They are formed of a few thick, large, fleshy scales. The styles are trifid and the ovary lobes and seedpods are winged.

3 THERESIA

F. persica is clearly a distinct species and is given its own group heading. It is a plant of western Asia. The bulb is large and long, usually of one dominant scale, the whole being probably wrapped in a light tunic, the remains of previous years' scales. It is many-flowered, bearing up to three dozen blooms in a terminal raceme. The style is undivided.

4 RHINOPETALUM

This small group of closely related species is found in Asia, centred on Afghanistan and spreading to Iran and with *F. karelinii* growing both in central Afghanistan and western China. This species has solitary flowers, *F. bucharica* can have 3–15 and the others will usually have 3–4. The group is characterized by conspicuously large nectaries. Styles are either entire or gently inclined towards some threefold division.

5 KOROLKOWIA

This is the other monotypic group. *F. sewerzowii* is a distinct plant that has in the past been thought sufficiently different by a Russian botanist to be made into a separate genus, *Korolkowia*. Until recently there has been little or no support for this view, though it is now gaining ground. *F. sewerzowii* is a central Asian species originally found in the Turkestan mountains. It can grow 45cm (18 inches) high, with 8–10 flowers. Normal styles are entire, but some flowers may be devoid of styles altogether.

6 LILIORHIZA

The varied plants in this section are restricted to North America, where they are most numerous in the Great Valley of California, except for *F. camschatcensis*, which ranges from California and Oregon through British Columbia to Alaska and over the Bering Straits into Asia. The bulbs are normally hard and disc-shaped, formed of imbricate (tightly overlapping) scales. A

SEED PODS

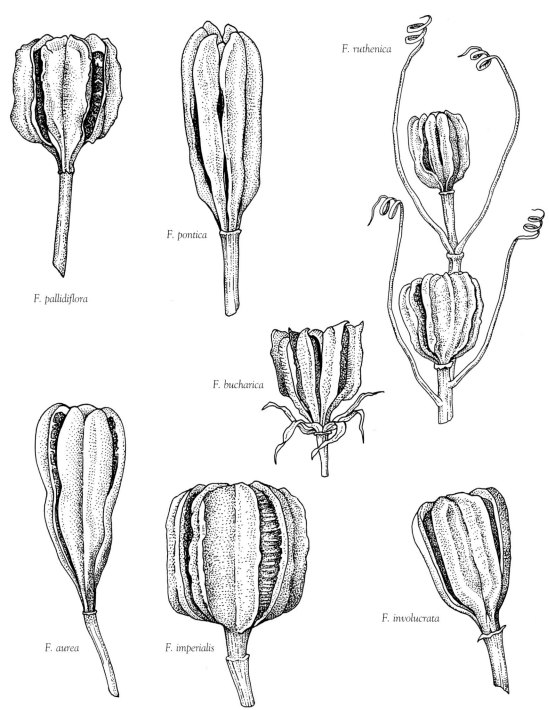

F. pallidiflora

F. pontica

F. ruthenica

F. bucharica

F. aurea

F. imperialis

F. involucrata

good proportion of these American species are characterized by having small bulblets on their outer surfaces, commonly called 'rice grains' because of their shape and small size. In many species they are found all over the surface, though in some they are more likely to be around the base only. While the norm is a single flower, some, especially the stronger bulbs, may have two or, rarely, three flowers; *F. camschatcensis* may have 8–9 on a stem, *F. pluriflora* may have 12 and *F. brandegeei* 7–8. *F. agrestis* and *F. liliacea* can be expected to provide 3–6. There is no conformity in this section about style shape – in some it is clearly trifid, in others three-lobed and in some completely entire. Nor is there uniformity of style forms within a species; some clones may have entire ones while others show a greater or lesser degree of tripartite division.

TABLE OF *FRITILLARIA* SECTIONS

This table lists all the species that are likely to be encountered by the gardener. There are other species that are at present little known, such as those described by the Chinese but not yet seen outside China.

1 EUFRITILLARIA

GROUP A
- *F. delavayi*
- *F. latifolia*
- *F. meleagris*
- *F. pallidiflora*
- *F. tubiformis*

GROUP B
- *F. cirrhosa*
- *F. olgae*
- *F. regelii*
- *F. thunbergii*

GROUP C
- *F. acmopetala*
- *F. crassifolia*
- *F. davisii*
- *F. epirotica*
- *F. graeca*
- *F. hermonis*
- *F. involucrata*
- *F. japonica*
- *F. kotschyana*
- *F. lusitanica*
- *F. messanensis*
- *F. michailovskyi*
- *F. montana*
- *F. olivieri*
- *F. pontica*
- *F. pyrenaica*
- *F. reuteri*
- *F. rhodokanakis*
- *F. straussii*
- *F. tuntasia*
- *F. whittallii*

GROUP D
- *F. alburyana*
- *F. alfredae*
- *F. armena*
- *F. assyriaca*
- *F. bithynica*
- *F. chlorantha*
- *F. conica*
- *F. drenovskyi*
- *F. elwesii*
- *F. ehrhartii*
- *F. euboeica*
- *F. fleischeriana*
- *F. forbesii*
- *F. minima*
- *F. latakiensis*
- *F. minuta*
- *F. obliqua*
- *F. pinardii*
- *F. rhodia*
- *F. sibthorpiana*
- *F. stribrnyi*
- *F. uva-vulpis*

2 PETILIUM

- *F. chitralensis*
- *F. eduardii*
- *F. imperialis*
- *F. raddeana*

3 THERESIA

- *F. persica*

4 RHINOPETALUM

- *F. ariana*
- *F. bucharica*
- *F. gibbosa*
- *F. karelinii*
- *F. stenanthera*

5 KOROLKOWIA

- *F. sewerzowii*

6 LILIORHIZA

GROUP A
- *F. camschatcensis*

GROUP B
- *F. agrestis*
- *F. biflora*
- *F. liliacea*
- *F. purdyi*

GROUP C
- *F. affinis*
- *F. atropurpurea*
- *F. brandegeei*
- *F. falcata*
- *F. glauca*

GROUP D
- *F. micrantha*
- *F. phaeanthera*
- *F. recurva*
- *F. viridia*

GROUP E
- *F. pudica*

GROUP F
- *F. pluriflora*
- *F. striata*

3

BUYING & CULTIVATING FRITILLARIES

There is only a limited period for buying fritillaries as dry bulbs and this is towards the end of the summer, when garden centres are just gearing themselves up for their annual autumn bulb festival. There may be some fritillaries among the first bulbs to be displayed and certainly one ought to buy as early as possible; a packet of 10–20 *F. meleagris* bulbs will be reasonably priced, but if this same packet has been on the shelf for several weeks it is going to be less of a bargain as some of the bulbs may have succumbed to bruising and fungal infection and be dead. It pays to look, purchase and plant early.

Its popularity makes *F. michailovskyi* one of the most readily available species in garden centres, where it will feature among the glut of autumn bulbs.

A wide range of fritillaries is not to be found in every garden centre. A few are readily available at such outlets and their number will probably increase steadily as bulb growers bulk up stocks through micro-propagation and also by field culture. At present the commercial leaders in this field at the Dutch producers, who market most of their products as prepacks complete with attractive coloured illustrations to tempt the buyer. At present garden centres can offer such species as *F. imperialis lutea*, *F. i. rubra*, *F. meleagris*, *F. michailovskyi* and *F. persica*.

Other places to buy dry bulbs are the autumn horticultural shows such as the ones at the Royal Horticultural Society halls at Westminster and those at Harrogate and Malvern. At the RHS gardens at Wisley there is a garden centre where there will be a wider range of species than is the norm at other garden centres – it may be possible to find well over a dozen species apart from the ones already listed.

If you set out to amass as complete a collection as possible you will soon realize that no one trader or nurseryman is going to be able to fulfil all your needs. The catalogues of bulb dealers may contain a selection of fritillaries but often the list can be limited to about half a dozen. More comprehensive lists are to be obtained from some of the more specialist growers, probably describing and perhaps illustrating up to 30 kinds. Do get a copy of their catalogues early – fritillaries are becoming very popular, and even at the quite substantial prices of some of them they can sell out early as stocks of many species are limited. It is worth contacting alpine specialists too as many of these will grow some fritillaries even if they do not list them in their catalogues. If they do feature in the catalogue a

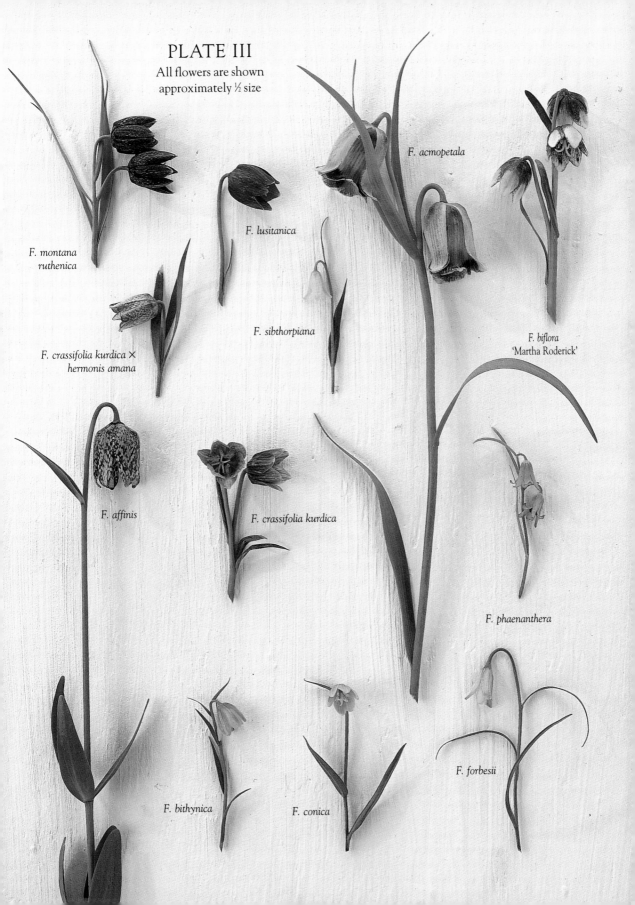

PLATE III
All flowers are shown
approximately ½ size

F. acmopetala

F. lusitanica

*F. montana
ruthenica*

*F. crassifolia kurdica ×
hermonis amana*

F. sibthorpiana

*F. biflora
'Martha Roderick'*

F. affinis

F. crassifolia kurdica

F. phaenanthera

F. bithynica

F. conica

F. forbesii

telephone call or note asking whether any others are available will often bring rewards.

You may find limited numbers of fritillaries for sale as potted plants at spring flower shows and at least you will know that you are picking a healthy plant when you can see the promising green shoots. Normally you will be safe in assuming that they are correctly labelled, but this is not always the case; without any intention to deceive, growers may have their bulbs wrongly named.

There is of course the uncommercial market economy to be tried. Fortunately the majority of fritillary amateurs have generous hearts and are ready to swop this plant for that. Alpine Garden Society members, especially those who enjoy showing, are very likely to have a small (or not so small) stable of fritillaries potted and in training for competition. If you join the AGS the flourishing local groups will enable you to see more plants and gardens than you would otherwise be able to do. The lily group of the RHS includes fritillaries and is another possible source of names of growers, plus a membership list with addresses which will enable you to see whether there are likely to be fanciers nearby. An added advantage of acquiring plants via these societies is that seasonal availability is not so limited. One of the difficulties in obtaining bulbs from mail order sources is that they often arrive in late autumn, long after the ideal planting time to give them their best chance of establishing quickly has passed. Joining specialist societies such as the AGS may make it possible to obtain plants at more sensible times from fellow enthusiasts who realize the importance of planting in late summer.

CHOOSING BULBS

The species that are offered for sale as dry bulbs in the late summer or early autumn are very likely to be among the easier and more reliable ones – the 'starter collection' on page 10 will guide your choice if you are new to the genus. Bulbs are often displayed either loose or in see-through packets so that you are able to choose the individual bulbs. Common sense comes into play here. Avoid damaged ones and any showing extensive mould. (A little blue penicillin mould may not rule out a bulb but it could be an indication of bruising or some other damage.) All other things being equal, a good big one beats a good little one. Some American kinds are likely to have 'rice grains' attached or shaken to the bottom of the receptacle, and these will form an embryo

stock waiting to be grown on. Other species may have attached bulblets too, if these have not been appropriated by the growers for propagation. Often traders will be offering three bulbs of a kind at a useful discount, and certainly three plants give an effect way beyond the rational formula of three times one.

CARE IN STORAGE

The place for fritillaries is in the soil, even if for many kinds this is best dry through the summer months. Deep under ground the bulbs are at a more or less constant temperature and are also protected from chance physical damage followed by fungoid infection. Large hardy kinds such as *F. imperialis* and *F. persica* are strong enough to stand the rather casual handling that often occurs in garden centres, but even these bruise relatively easy and are subject to serious deterioration out of the ground. Others, especially the ones with small bulbs, can begin to suffer quite quickly if left exposed to drying and varying temperatures. If you have bulbs of any species out of the ground for some good purpose, they are best rinsed or dusted with fungicide, carefully labelled and covered in peat or similar material that has some moisture but is dry rather than sodden.

OUTDOORS OR INDOORS?

Some fritillaries come from parts of the world where they may never experience frost when actively growing or they may be so adapted to long dry summers that the wet we often experience can prove fatal to them. These will require protection. Other kinds are as hardy as possible, and indeed *F. meleagris* does grow wild in a few localities in the United Kingdom. There are some species that, while being suited to pots, may do as well or even better outside provided the right spot is chosen.

GARDEN SITES

All the crown imperials – that is, all the species falling into section 2 – are prime candidates for the herbaceous or mixed border, being large enough to make a real contribution to the late spring and early summer display. Size alone ensures that *F. imperialis* will not be overlooked, especially as the bulbs increase and large clumps are formed. In the smaller garden it might even be necessary to restrict oneself to the shorter kinds that only reach a height of 60–91cm (24–36 inches). This category includes the dramatic *F. i.* 'Prolifera'

PLATE IV
All flowers are approximately ⅓ size

F. imperialis lutea

F. imperialis aurora

F. imperialis rubra

(Crown-on-Crown) with its two or three rings of orange bells not usually topping more than 60cm (24 inches), and *F. i.* 'Lutea', with yellow flowers and a maximum height of 91cm (36 inches).

Newly planted crown imperials can disappoint by blooming their first year but only producing leaves the following season. We can offer a set of rules that should produce a reasonable rate of increase and reliable flowering, but we know that not everyone's experience will be the same. The first point is the most contentious.

1 The large bulbs have a central hole where the previous year's stem has died away. The much-repeated advice is that bulbs should be planted somewhat on their side so that in their summer resting period water will not be encouraged to gather here and rot the bulbs. Some people, however, argue that even if bulbs are planted on their side it only takes the plant a season to right itself and it is thereafter normally level anyway.

2 Plant bulbs deeply, with 25–45 cm (10–18 inches) of soil over their tops, in well-worked free-draining loam or garden soil in good heart.

3 Put a bucketful of grit below a group of bulbs to encourage the drainage that is so important at all times and to give an extra dryness to the summer period.

4 Give plenty of humus-rich material as an annual mulch together with a scatter of general fertilizer and, ideally, give liquid feeds during

F. ehrhartii, a species from Greece, comes into growth early and may welcome the shelter of a bulb frame.

the growing period (late winter or early spring) and again once or twice up to flowering time.

5 Fritillary roots should never be disturbed as they do not regrow once broken, so take care not to damage them with hoe, fork or spade. Most failures are caused by disturbance or by planting that is too shallow. Once leaf growth has died back, in early to midsummer, the roots will be finished and bulbs can be examined and replanted.

There are plenty of other species that will grow well in borders, often needing no attention at all but perhaps doing better with a little help. Most of the European species can be grown towards the front of beds or borders. On the whole these kinds can cope with a plentiful supply of water through the spring and even through the winter if the soil is an open-structured one with free drainage. They will be quite happy through summer with some moisture but will be just as content if the soil dries out for a while, though they are not among the species that benefit from a really hot baking, preferring to be reasonably cool at bulb level. These species are: *F. armena*; *F. conica*; *F. davisii*; *F. drenovskii*; *F. ehrhartii*; *F. graeca*; *F. involucrata*; *F. latifolia*; *F. lusitanica*; *F. meleagris*; *F. messanensis*; *F. montana*; *F. obliqua*; *F. pontica*; *F. pyrenaica*; *F. rhodokanakis*; *F. sibthorpiana*; *F. stribrnyi*; *F. tubiformis* and *F. tuntasia*.

The traditional herbaceous border undergoes considerable upheaval every year or alternate years. This does not suit fritillaries, but pure herbaceous borders are now very few; mixed borders with herbaceous plants, shrubs and bulbs are popular instead. Fritillaries associate with dwarf shrubs very well (see Chapter 4), thriving on the stability and dappled shade they provide. Shrubs also help to keep the soil drier through the summer by virtue of the sheltering leaf canopy and the roots taking up moisture. Fritillaries that enjoy the open life outside but may well be happier with some light shade include such useful species as *F. affinis*, *F. camschatcensis*, *F. elwesii*, *F. graeca*, *F. imperialis*, *F. involucrata*, *F. lusitanica*, *F. obliqua*, *F. pallidiflora*, *F. pontica*, *F. thunbergii*, *F. tuntasia*.

Even in beds there will be differing micro-climates and soil conditions. Towards a sloped front facing the sun there can be places where the soil really gets quite a

F. graeca, from northern Greece and Bulgaria, is a variable species but usually does well in British gardens.

baking in the summer – perhaps not on a level of some spots in the eastern Mediterranean basin but often enough to allow some of the more amenable species from this area to be tried. Certainly *F. acmopetala*, *F. assyriaca*, *F. bithynica*, *F. crassifolia*, *F. elwesii*, *F. pallidiflora* and *F. whitallii* might be planted with a good likelihood of complete success. If your pot-grown *F. conica* stock increases it might be worth trying one or two outside, and this is a strategy that you may wish to try with others that you grow with protection. You may find that your garden suits species that are marked 'for under glass only'.

Heather gardens or beds are excellent for fritillaries as they offer a relatively stable environment that is likely to be well-drained and open to sunshine. Here you could try some of the eastern Europeans and even Asiatics such as *F. persica* and *F. pallidiflora*. Heathers

F. obliqua is a rare plant in cultivation and is only just holding on in its wild habitats in Greece.

F. elwesii is a graceful little plant from the great heartland of fritillaries, south-western Turkey, where it is found growing in pine woodlands.

are normally associated with the acid soil conditions that suit many fritillaries, but many very successful heather gardens have been constructed on neutral or even somewhat alkaline soils; it is the particularly valuable winter-flowering forms of *Erica carnea* and *E.* × *darleyensis* that are lime-tolerant. As the vast majority of gardens hover close to the neutral mark on the pH scale it is relatively easy to adjust areas to be a little more acidic or alkaline as required.

while others will favour a higher degree of humus and more acid conditions. Fritillaries can be slotted into such spots, preferably combined with small twiggy shrubs or not-too-dominant alpines to give stem support. Many species from Turkey and the Balkans and perhaps even some of the Caucasian and Afghanistan kinds are suitable for a place in the rock garden, including *F. bithynica*, *F. chlorantha*, *F. crassifolia* and *F. drenoskyi*.

Climatic factors are tricky to pin down. The sunshine of the Middle East is in a different class to that of the Lake District, for example, and a species that may benefit from some shade in East Anglia is unlikely to need the equivalent of a parasol to protect it from overexposure to the sun in Cumbria and along the west coast of Scotland. Common sense is the answer here.

In the wild many species are found on screes, clearly showing the preference of the genus for drainage before

Perhaps the most obvious place for fritillaries grown outdoors is the rock garden or rock bed. There will certainly be sun-baked spots, as the first rule about rock gardens is that they should be sited in the open away from shade cast by trees and buildings. There are likely to be slopes that do not face the sun fully and these may even have a few corners behind a rock or small shrub which have a little shade. Most importantly, any moderately well-constructed rock garden will have one thing fritillaries favour – open-textured, well-drained soil. Standing water is a death sentence to fritillaries. Some pockets of a rock garden will have excessively fine drainage,

F. acmopetala is an easy garden plant and a weed in the fields of the Eastern Mediterranean countries. The yellowish form shown here is less common than those with maroon shading.

F. whitallii looks like a large snake's head fritillary; the clone shown here is paler than most. This species is from rocky places in south-western Turkey, and is easy to cultivate in pots or in the bulb frame.

all else. Some gardens may run to a scree bed perhaps as part of, or an adjunct to, the rock garden. Virtually all the small fritillaries would welcome such a site, though some may want the humus content increasing and some will be happier with water running below, particularly *F. alburyana* and *F. camschatcensis*.

Troughs and other containers such as half-tubs are suitable for some species. A miniature landscape such as in a sink garden will house a community of plants that demand first-rate drainage and yet will not stand for complete desiccation in the summer. Many small fritillaries will fit in here, having discreet foliage, flower stems that do not lengthen inordinately when producing seed and neat seedpods.

Fritillaries to grow in a rock bed or a trough include *F. affinis*, *F. armena*, *F. biflora*, *F. cirrhosa*, *F. davisii*, *F. latifolia*, *F. meleagris*, *F. pyrenaica*, *F. rhodokanakis* and *F. tubiformis*.

F. crassifolia kurdica is an early-flowering dwarf plant, represented here by a dark clone; others will have yellow lips and central green stripes.

NATURALIZING BULBS

There are several species that can be expected to flourish for decades when planted in light grass or very light woodland. The obvious example is the snake's head fritillary, *F. meleagris*, which can be seen in a few protected British sites. At Cricklade in Gloucestershire, not far from the source of the Thames, there is one large water meadow which in late spring is covered with a pattern of mauve and white fritillaries and golden dandelions. Many gardeners must have tried to emulate these conditions on a smaller scale. The best bet is a patch of light grass in a damp spot, mown severely in the autumn or early winter and then left until midsummer before being brought low again. It is virtually impossible to see the growth of the bulbs in spring as their stems and foliage merge so completely with the grass; it is only when the buds suddenly open that they make their presence felt. When the flowers fade the plants are again lost to sight and it is at this stage there is a temptation to

tidy the grass. However, this must be resisted as the fritillaries will all be cut down and the plants weakened; it only needs this to happen two or three times for a colony to be wiped out.

Other European species can be tried in light grass, including *F. caucasica*, *F. involucrata*, *F. latifolia*, *F. lusitanica*, *F. messanensis* and *F. pyrenaica*. The crown imperials can be tried in open situations in the wild garden, again taking care to allow the stems and foliage to die down in their own time.

GARDEN SOILS

Most gardens can support most hardy fritillaries. On the whole they will grow in a range of pH values around the neutral mark; acid/alkali preferences are given in the A–Z list in this book. The type of soil conditions in which they are found growing in the wild is an obvious guide to cultural needs, but such information has to be used sensibly (see Chapter 6). It is not possible to mirror the wild conditions exactly, but if one basic type of garden soil had to be created to suit the majority it would be a deep loam with perhaps an equal volume of rocky grit. The texture ought to be open. Species that grow in quite different wild conditions will probably settle down to this domestic recipe quite happily. Of course there are exceptions – some of the American species that come from clay grasslands that dry out almost to brick hardness in the summer may need a heavier, more compact soil to feel at home.

Shown here is one of the new cultivars of *F. meleagris*, a fine plant called 'Pink Eveline'.

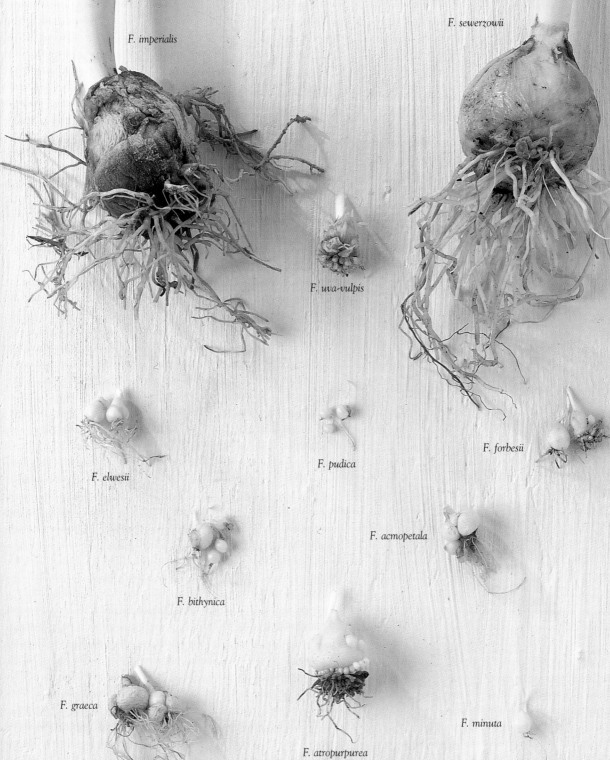

PLATE V
All bulbs are shown approximately full size

F. imperialis

F. sewerzowii

F. uva-vulpis

F. elwesii

F. pudica

F. forbesii

F. acmopetala

F. bithynica

F. graeca

F. atropurpurea

F. minuta

PREPARING SITES

The importance of all other factors fade into relative insignificance compared with the need to protect bulbs from an excess of water, especially in the long period after flowering until the autumn. A healthy soil has a structure that allows surplus water to drain down and away, retaining enough moisture for plant roots to flourish. With many plants the most important rooting areas are in the first few centimetres but, left to their own devices, fritillary bulbs tend to tuck themselves down into the ground surprisingly deeply, perhaps as a precaution against fluctuating temperatures around their rootrun. It follows that attention to drainage means delving deeply unless the soil profile is one that naturally allows water to pass very freely. This can be tackled by raising the soil level of the planting sites and double digging to allow more air into lower levels.

Heavy soils will benefit from the addition of rubble and hardcore in the second spit, and if there is a serious threat of water being retained for any extended time it would be sensible to lay field drains to a lower area, an efficient sump or a more major drain. The topsoil may be made more gritty and an addition of leaf mould or other humus will help many species. Special requirements are given in the A–Z list.

PLANTING

The timing of planting depends when the bulbs become available. Home-grown bulbs can be planted early – midsummer or when the flowers have faded and the leaves are just going. However, it is not always easy to get bulbs from suppliers so early as garden centres and other sources tend to bracket fritillaries with all the autumn bulbs. Specialist growers may be rather better in this regard. The rule is to plant as early as possible, as even those species with a long summer rest period will do better with an early start.

Planting depths vary according to the species and the size of its bulbs. The temptation is to plant too shallowly, but no species would be happy with less than about 10cm (4 inches) of soil covering them. The larger the bulb the deeper it goes, with the crown imperials and *F. persica* bulbs having perhaps 25–45cm (10–18 inches) over the top.

Many, if not most, fritillaries benefit from a large handful of grit (a bucketful when planting a group), to help to keep them dry through the summer and pro-

mote the rooting process after, but this is dependent on the whole site being properly drained.

CARE

If your fritillaries are planted in the correct conditions there is very little else for you to do except admire the blossom. Some species will enjoy a top dressing of well-rotted compost each year, and certainly weeds should be kept in check. More important is to watch the growth of neighbouring plants – while one of the best sites for many kinds is in the lee of a deciduous shrub, shrubs grow and what was a useful light twiggy support and shelter to start with can very quickly become an impenetrable mass that will thwart the aspiring stems. The bulbs will need moving or the shrub pruning – preferably the latter, given that fritillaries dislike being moved and disturbed.

Clean culture, gritty soils and a pair of sharp eyes can help to keep the slug population to a minimum. You should certainly do what you can to keep their numbers down, especially in the late winter and early spring, when the optimum activity of slugs coincides with the most crucial growing period for fritillaries. Slug traps of stale beer or your own favoured methods can be combined with applications of the newer slug baits that are harmless to pets and wildlife. These slug pellets work best in moist conditions but may need topping up after prolonged heavy rain.

If you are trying outdoor cultivation of some of the species that are normally grown under glass and benefit from summer drought, it could save life and encourage further flowering next season if you provide cover with a cloche or a sheet of polythene, extending it well beyond the bulbs' site and securing and disguising it with a scatter of compost or shredded bark. Obviously you will need to remember to remove it when the summer is over.

DIVISION

While some species are exceedingly slow to increase naturally, there are plenty that quite quickly establish robust clumps. These will need lifting and dividing before they become so crowded as to lose their flowering potential. The time to do this is while you can still see the foliage but it is turning or has turned beige. Lift the clumps carefully, place the whole clods of soil on a sheet of plastic or a proper garden-tidy and gently break

F. *michailovskyi* Multiform is the most unusual form of this amenable species. Its many-headed flower stems force the blooms towards the horizontal giving it a totally distinct character from the strictly pendant type.

away the soil and rescue the bulbs. Do not put these into storage unless you have some good reason for doing so; it is better to replant the separated bulbs in fresh positions which you have dug over and prepared ready for them, remembering to label them clearly.

POT CULTURE

There are three good reasons for growing some bulbs in pots: first, they may be enjoyed at close quarters more easily than when they are grown outdoors, which is no mean consideration with some of the very small early-flowering kinds; secondly, some of the species come into growth early and are not frost hardy; and thirdly, British

summers are often wet and there are a number of species from semi-deserts, screes and mountain slopes, where they expect to be kept very dry after flowering until the autumn. A lot of rain can injure or kill these.

All fritillaries can be grown under protection but here we concentrate on the conditions for those that really need extra help, such as some of the American species. The kind of protection needed is that provided by a cold greenhouse, an alpine house, a conservatory and/or a cold frame or bulb frame. Heating is not required, except that sufficient to keep the relatively few frost-tender kinds safe.

Clay pots are preferred for many plants because they allow more air to the soil and are less likely to get sodden. Nevertheless, the comparison of results of clay and plastic pot-grown fritillaries over a period of several years has seemed to prove the point that plastic may be best for these plants; bulbs have increased appreciably faster, flower count has been higher and there seems also to have been a better harvest of seed capsules. This is the experience of more than one grower and although it goes in the face of what most people might naturally assume, it seems that properly mixed compost and correct water management have provided a more equable soil environment and temperature and moisture levels have been more beneficially stable.

It is best to use rather large pots – not less than 15cm (6 inches) and perhaps even slightly larger to give the desired depth. The larger mass of soil means that it is more likely to keep within narrow degrees of fluctuation in terms of both moisture and temperature than is possible in small pots. There should be good drainage holes that can be covered with pieces of perforated plastic or metal to keep out unwanted animal life and to allow water to drain freely from the gritty mix. A basic mix might be, by volume: 2 parts good grade sterilized loam/2 parts very coarse washed sand or grit/1 part humus as coarse peat or similar material. Add a sprinkling of general fertilizer.

A group of three plants will have a much greater impact than a single fritillary in a large pot, while 10–12 plants of one of the smaller species in a 20cm (8 inch) pot can look very impressive. The bulbs should be at least 8–10cm (3–4 inches) deep and, once planted, can be given a thorough soaking before being allowed to drain and then accommodated on a bench which has capillary matting or a plunge material of washed grit at least halfway up the pot. This can help to keep temperature and moisture levels even.

If the plants are potted in the late summer, the pots can then be kept just moist and cool without frost until the shoots appear in the late winter and early spring, when a more generous watering regime can be allowed. Two or three mild liquid feeds will not come amiss when plants are in full growth. Tomato fertilizers are high in potash, the most important of elements, but the strength of the feed should be very dilute – only a third or a quarter used for ordinary plants – and this should be applied only to mature plants that have been several seasons in the same pot. Young bulbs seem to do very much better nurtured on clean water, with the soil mix providing the nutrients needed. However, probably more fritillaries are lost through overwatering rather than underwatering, so do not be overenthusiastic in this regard.

ROUND-YEAR ROUTINE

Repotting may be undertaken as the foliage fails. The stronger plants may have bulblets that you can grow on separately, preferably repotting them immediately. However, it is not necessary to be in a hurry to repot, as the bulbs are often best left without interference for three or four years until they become crowded. The top soil can be scraped away annually to a depth of 7.5cm (3 inches) and replenished with fresh. This should be done delicately, as bulbs are not necessarily static and you could cause damage if you assumed otherwise. Old soil can be worked into an area of the garden where any bulblets that you failed to spot can grow.

If they are planted initially in a large pot some species, including the American ones, may well perform better if left relatively untouched for many years until the pot is obviously no longer big enough. The top few centimetres of soil can be replaced with fresh on an annual basis. When you are handling these American species you may be tempted to remove all or most of the rice grain bulblets to increase your stock. This may be a mistake, as parent bulbs seem to resent a wholesale loss of bulblets and show this by a diminution of flowering potential. Take only a few bulblets and leave the rest in situ.

A few weeks after flowering some species begin to flag. At this point watering can be reduced and those species needing a thorough baking placed in a suitable position such as on a shelf of the greenhouse. Many of them can be placed outside in a frame which can be left open in good weather and closed down in very wet periods. Start pots into growth with a light watering in the autumn.

BULB BEDS & FRAMES

A large proportion of fritillaries from warmer areas thrive in bulb beds, and anyone trying to accumulate a wide collection needs such a bed or something close to it. In a bulb bed some kinds will flourish that would normally struggle or fail, and another important advantage is that bulbs grown in these beds may multiply at a dramatically increased rate.

There is no special magic about these beds – the main feature is the improved drainage, usually arranged by heightening the soil levels and containing them with brick, stone or railway sleeper walls. Soil mixes can be manipulated, and a useful general mix is the same or

PLATE VI
Flowers are shown approximately full size

F. alfredae glaucoviridis

F. drenovskii

F. uva-vulpis

F. persica

similar to that recommended above for potting, used over a layer of hardcore.

A further stage along this cultural route is the bulb frame, a sort of hybrid between a normal cold frame and a small greenhouse. This allows tight control over the water content of the soil – you can instigate an artificial drought in the summer and make the winter less of a lengthy period of sodden misery which may prove fatal to fritillaries. The sides are built up, a soil mix can be chosen to ensure perfect drainage and there is an option of covering the top with glass.

A bulb frame is very easy to construct. Choose a site that is light, preferably sheltered from the worst of the winds, and of easy access so that water, wheelbarrows and tools can be brought within working distance and you will have room to move. The width of the frame should be no wider than can comfortably reached from the side or sides; the length is a matter of choice. Height is also a matter of convenience and aesthetics. Five courses of bricks above ground level will bring the top to around 38cm (15in); you may feel that a three-course level of approximately 20cm (8in) will look better and it will certainly take less filling! Railway sleepers give instant walls – one on its side will certainly be deep enough. If bending down poses a problem, you could make the height equivalent to that of a table at 75cm (30in).

The walls should allow for drainage at the bottom. If they are of stone or brick the choice is yours as to whether you make them secure with mortaring or go for a more informal dry-stone effect. Whatever you decide, it will preclude any future disappointment if the soil mix inside is made as rodent-proof as possible. To exclude mice and others the bottom, sides and ends of the frame need lining with a fine grade galvanized wire mesh, with no holes at the corners or elsewhere; mice can squeeze through very small holes and once through can create havoc by eating the bulbs and building nests. Bring the mesh up to the top of the wall and lay a framed sheet of mesh across the top to prevent ingress, especially in the months from autumn through the winter. Cloche-like glass tops that can be securely wired or otherwise joined to the walls will complete the top. It will be a considerable bonus if the glass is easily removable.

You will need a layer of hardcore drainage, topped with a compost mix that comes to within some 8–10cm (3–4 inches) of the wall tops. This allows a little growing space before requiring the removal of the protective top mesh sheet. The aim is to have sufficient soil mix for the bulbs to be planted some 10–20cm (4–8 inches) deep and still have some rooting space below.

It is easiest to have a rather more generously proportioned frame than you may originally think sufficient. This is because if bulbs of fritillaries and other genera are planted directly into the soil mix they will not remain completely static and labelling, while correct at the time of planting, can become less and less dependable as the plants grow. One bulb may look very much like another bulb of a related kind when they are lifted, so you need to try to keep species separate. This can mean planting different species well apart and using the space between for plants of other genera.

Another ploy is to surround each group of bulbs of a particular species within a horizontal cordon of fine mesh plastic such as is often used for bagging smaller fruits in supermarkets. Alternatively, try the plastic pots used for aquatic plants, which have the sides and base generously cut away to allow free flow of water. The mesh or pot should prevent too much invasion, but do not rely on this completely – rice grains and stoloniferous growth may breech the cordon, though this usually occurs only when the netting is damaged. To make absolutely sure movement is restricted, you could completely line the sites of American species with the rice grain habit, as well as others that produce small bulbils freely, with a bag of very fine plastic mesh before adding the soil mix and placing the bulbs in position. At lifting time the bulbs can be removed as a bagful with their attendant soil and then the bulbs carefully sorted out on a plastic sheet well clear of neighbours. Even so, it is surprisingly easy when you are transferring used soil to other spots of the garden to unwittingly transplant bulbs which will appear the following season.

The bulb frame with its winter protection is suitable for some potted bulbs – the overflow from the cold greenhouse or alpine house or species that do not need the complete frostproofing offered there but are still not quite hardy enough to be grown outside. Pots can be kept cool and safe here during summer periods, suiting species not needing the warmth and drought they would experience under the permanent cover of a greenhouse or alpine house.

4
PLANT ASSOCIATIONS

It is not difficult to find plants to associate with fritillaries, the majority of species being relatively small and unobtrusive. It is only the crown imperials that are capable of making a strong statement and need to be given an extra bit of space. In the wild fritillaries can be found in high mountain fastnesses with little close company, but more usually they grow among other plants which often provide support for the rather modest stems of some fritillaries.

THE WILD GARDEN

The most freely available of the species is *F. meleagris*, a pasture or meadowland plant in many places, but also found in thin scrub or woodland. It does well as part of a managed wild garden, which is to say growing in light grass that does not get mown until the seed pods ripen in the first half of the summer. Grow it with a variety of native plants such as early primroses (*Primula vulgaris*), slightly later cowslips (*P. veris*), bluebells (*Hyacinthoides non-scripta*), viper's bugloss (*Echium vulgare*), and such jolly little leguminous plants as birdsfoot trefoil (*Lotus corniculatus*). The grasses themselves may form the unifying theme, but avoid coarse couch grasses or other broad-leaved strong species and plant such species as fescues, bents and Good Friday grass (*Carex humilis*), a miniature sedge which only grows to some 7.5cm (3 inches) high.

The wild garden is not necessarily the easiest type of garden to cultivate – woodland is rather easier as the trees and shrubs exert their influence more steadily on

F. stenanthera is an unorthodox Asian species which starts into growth early and does best with the protection of a bulb frame or an alpine house.

The popular snake's head fritillary, *F meleagris*, here growing happily in woodland.

the environment. In the rougher parts of any wild area of grass-cum-scrub it is possible to grow some peonies provided they can see the sun, and the same applies to the crown imperials. The peonies will last for decades, as will *F. imperialis* given at the very least 20cm

A fine stand of the vigorous golden form of the crown imperial, *F. imperialis lutea*. Only 100 years after *F. imperialis* was introduced there were 30 different forms available.

(8 inches) of soil over the bulb tops. On the edge of light woodland you can expect *F. meleagris* and other species such as *F. armena*, *F. latifolia*, *F. lusitanica*, *F. involucrata*, *F. affinis* and *F. pallidiflora* to grow easily enough. Plant *Anemone nemorosa*, *A. apennina* and *A. blanda* for early company. Some of the more interesting forms of the lady fern (*Athyrium filix-femina*) would provide contrasting foliage and take up surplus water later in the season, which would help to keep the fritillary bulbs from being swamped.

The base of a large tree is a good site for a collection of plants that complete their growing period between autumn and late spring. Both autumn- and spring-flowering crocuses will manage here well enough, as will long-lived hardy cyclamens such as *Cyclamen hederifolium*, *C. coum* and *C. repandum*. You can plant the

fritillaries listed in the previous paragraph and also *F. acmopetala* and *F. pyrenaica*. Indeed, such spots have what most fritillaries need – sunlight and moisture in the early part of the year but a little light shade later and relative drought through the summer, caused by the partial leaf canopy and the moisture-sucking roots.

The type of tree is not important except that it should be deciduous. Although in the wild fritillaries are often found growing in pine forests, these are not normally dense forests but rather landscapes where pines, though the most important constituent of the vegetation, are scattered with plenty of space between. Fritillaries are not going to survive under the dense growth of garden conifers such as *Chamaecyparis lawsoniana* forms. Most obviously decorative would be a maple (*Acer*), but if you are planting a new tree you will have to wait a few years for any of this genus to reach a decent height.

F. bithynica, a species from the Eastern Mediterranean, here looking well established in normal garden conditions.

F. lusitanica, a plant that is sometimes hard to come by as it hybridizes freely with *F. pyrenaica.*

ROCK GARDENS, ROCK BEDS & TROUGHS

The most obvious spot for many of the small species that can be grown outside is in a rock garden, rock bed or trough garden. Groups of fritillaries can look just right here in niches by rocks or growing in close association with thymes (*Thymus*), the smaller hebes, small brooms (*Genista* or *Cytisus* forms), dwarf rhododendrons, daphnes, dwarf phloxes or helianthemums as well as a whole variety of sub-shrubby plants that may help shelter and support the bulbs. Sempervivums, saxifragas, sedums and campanulas will provide contrasting forms. If fritillaries are grown next to clumps of anemones such as *Anemone blanda* the differences of habit will highlight the characters of both; it makes good sense to try to position fritillaries in such a way as to emphasize their unique qualities. Rocks and gravel will help in this too.

Trough gardens and rock beds will suit many small fritillaries that enjoy open sunshine, good drainage and a summer that will not be as arid as some species may like because there are other plants to care for. This includes most of the small European species, which will look delightful with pretty small plants such as

encrusted saxifragas *Saxifraga* 'Tumbling Waters' or *S. longifolia, Primula marginata* and other dainty primroses, *Gentiana saxosa* and some small geraniums such as *Geranium cinereum* cultivars and the more compact forms of *G. sanguineum,* for example 'Shepherd's Warning' or 'Glenluce'.

HEATHER BEDS

Heather beds planted with forms of *Erica carnea* and *E. × darleyensis* spaced so as to allow room for bulbs in between will look effective. Small tulips and early-flowering dwarf narcissi make bright contrasts to the heathers; you could also plant the choicer muscari species, scillas and ornithogalums, though you will have to take care that the latter do not become too invasive. *Muscari botryoides* and its white form 'Album' are neat grape hyacinths that increase respectably but not invasively. *M. tubergenianum* is nicknamed the Oxford and Cambridge grape hyacinth as it has its lower flowers a very dark blue and the upper ones a paler shade. It too is a stocky species not given to excessively fast procreation. The very early pale blue *Scilla mischtschenkoana* will finish flowering long before any fritillaries grown outdoors but *S. bithynica,* with racemes of pale blue flowers on 20cm (8in) stems, may well be in bloom with *F. meleagris* and other species. *Ornithogalum umbellatum* is very invasive and perhaps *O. nutans,* standing 20–25cm (8–10 inches) high with pleasing flowerheads of silvery-white and green blooms arranged like a slim hyacinth, is a better choice. It can accompany many of the fritillaries in bloom, its rather unusual colouring not looking out of place among them.

Some of the smaller lilies will come into flower when the fritillaries have died right back or are merely faded standards topped with seedpods. These could include the hybrid Pixie series in many colours or species such as the orange *Lilium pumilum* or the dwarf white-trumpeted *L. formosanum* var. *pricei.*

A clump of *F. pallidiflora* standing perhaps 50cm (20 inches) tall can look very impressive above the heathers. *F. pontica* is equally tall and can be tucked in a spot which is likely to be kept a little cooler and moister through the summer. Amenable species such as *F. uva-vulpis* and *F. pyrenaica* will soon form good-sized clumps.

F. uva-vulpis grows and increases very freely in cultivation and will naturalize itself in damp soil.

F. elwesii is hardy and grows well but having a rather fragile stem will benefit from leaning a little on the heathers, its flowers protruding higher on stems around 30cm (12 inches) tall. It is a species close to the very prolific *F. acmopetala*, which grows 30–50cm (12–20 inches) high and is happy among the heathers and indeed many other plants – it can thrive towards the front of an orthodox herbaceous border or one of mixed herbaceous and shrubby plants. The heather bed or garden makes an ideal spot to try other species not so well known as easy garden plants.

SHRUBS

While fritillaries benefit from the support and shelter afforded by shrubs they cannot force themselves through very thick cover, nor can they survive long under such growth. It is the outer reaches of some shrubs that are ideal places, giving support without suffocation. Very strong-growing shrubs are not good partners, and only the most open of evergreen ones are suitable, for example lavenders, rosemaries and the lighter-weight cistuses.

Among the deciduous shrubs that could foster fritillaries the shrubby potentillas and brooms come to mind first. *Ceratostigma willmottianum* is just about the right fighting weight, a deciduous shrub growing some 0.6–1.2m (2–4ft) tall and rather wider, with plenty of relatively light branches reaching upwards and outwards. Its rich blue flowers are produced from midsummer until the frosts, providing interest when the fritillaries are dormant. Sometimes a hard winter cuts back growth but this scarcely matters as it is soon replaced. This shrub can flourish in dry conditions; it was found by Ernest Wilson growing in the arid, precipitous Min Valley in China which was also the sole home of *Lilium regale*, perhaps Wilson's most important introduction. Try planting fritillaries to the side and front of the shrub, with the more massive *L. regale* behind.

Fritillaries look well beside berberises or the popular coloured-stemmed dogwoods (*Cornus alba* forms), also from China. However, they can also be charming below native plants such as hazels or some of the smaller willows such as the lovely wide-leaved silver-grey *Salix lanata*.

FERNS

Ferns are usually thought of as plants for damp and shady places, but several species will grow in drier, more open areas; although none like uninterrupted sunshine,

some can manage without sopping wet soil and deep shade. The male fern (*Dryopteris filix-mas*), with many mutant forms, is one that will do well in a variety of sites; it is a robust plant with fronds over 60cm (2ft) long and is able to grow to over double this in ideal conditions. The polypodys are very drought-resistant, and there are forms of *Polypodium vulgare* and *P. australe* which are 10–40 cm (4–16 inches) high, according to site – useful sizes to accompany fritillaries.

MEDITERRANEAN BEDS

A series of drier, warmer summers has prompted the use of Mediterranean plants in British gardens. It seems to be assumed that the greenhouse effect will lead to a more restricted supply of summer moisture – not a worry for fritillary growers.

The Mediterranean bed needs to be sited in as sunny a position as possible, perhaps contoured to face the sun at a flatter angle and make drainage sharper. The planting does not have to be entirely Mediterranean, but could include all those plants that flourish in drier and warmer climates than the normal British one. *Cistus* species and hybrids come to mind, and also the useful silver-leaved *Brachyglottis* 'Sunshine' (syn. *Senecio* 'Sunshine'). Many of the plants from sunnier habitats help to conserve their moisture by restricting transpiration through the leaves, and to this end they are covered with a fine layer of hairs which give a silvery appearance. The wormwood *Artemisia absinthium* makes silvery-white mounds of foliage. Smaller plants such as *Anacyclus pyrethrum* var. *depressus* lie flat on the ground with grey-green cut foliage and wide-open daisy flowers. Between the shrubs and the alpine-type ground-huggers there are the South African osteospermums.

The roots of plants can be given some protection from heat and excessive dehydration by a layer of grit or pebbles over the surface. This certainly gives a sense of unity to the bed and one popular idea is to imitate the appearance of a dried river bed with sweeps of pebbles, perhaps of different sizes, and occasional larger boulders. Such sites are ideal for many fritillaries. As many species are found on mountain screes, parts of the Mediterranean bed could be made to mimic scree conditions, with much more grit than soil.

F. imperialis lutea grows quickly through the spring to bloom and then die back before the summer is much advanced.

5

PROPAGATION & BREEDING

All bulbous plants are expected by gardeners to be generous in their vegetative increase, but fritillaries do not always oblige so dramatically as some other bulbous genera; there are few that approach the fecundity of some muscari species and alliums. However, strong bulbs will divide and some, especially the American species, produce bulblets which can be grown on to flowering size at least one year quicker than plants raised from seed. Scales can be broken from the plant and propagated to produce a series of small bulblets to grow on. It has proven not difficult to mass-propagate some species by tissue culture (micro-propagation) but as this needs attention to detail and laboratory-type hygiene it is normally the province of specialized commercial technology.

However, undoubtedly the soundest and perhaps the most exciting method of propagation is by seed. This is normally abundantly produced – a full seedpod can easily have well in excess of 50 viable seeds so that a few plants could, in theory, give rise to large populations. There are few things in this world that compare with the joy and excitement of seeing a new batch of seedlings blooming for the first time, perhaps to grow into some fine plants. The main problem with this propagation method, however, is the patience that is required; some species will take 4–6 years to reach flowering status.

The advantages of vegetative propagation are that usually the units are larger, easier to handle, and will bloom somewhat earlier than plants from seed. Every propagated piece will give rise to plants and flowers identical to the vegetative parent, so you can take a particularly fine form and reproduce it exactly. Given the same conditions it will behave exactly like its parent, so it will bloom at the same time, at the same height and in the same colour.

The disadvantages of vegetative propagation are the converse of its virtues. There will be a lack of diversity – if there is a weak feature, all will have it. Should the original bulb used for propagation be infected by virus, all the plants grown from it after its infection will be similarly affected.

All seed-raised plants will start clear of any virus diseases, and there are other advantages. The resulting plants will provide a larger genetic pool; while plants of a species will be similar there can be important horticultural variations even from the progeny of a single pod. Flower colours and patterning may give a surprisingly wide choice in some species, and even the most orthodox species can vary a little. This may be only a matter of the amount of plum-like 'bloom' on the petals, but a touch extra can transform a beautiful flower into one that is outstanding. Features that immediately catch the eye are important, but there are others that can be just as vital; the strength of bulb growth is not a standard feature. It makes sense when raising plants from seed to select not only the best-looking ones but also the strong 'doers'.

SEED

Fritillary seed is similar to that of lilies, though often somewhat smaller. It consists of flat discs with a flat narrow fringe of dried wasted tissue around the more or less circular disc of lively cell tissue. It is from this centre that germination is signalled by the growth of the first shoot, called the radical. The seeds are not designed for long storage, so there are no strong protective shells or layers. They are meant to float or be blown from their

PLATE VII
All flowers shown approximately ⅓ size

seed capsules

F. imperialis prolifera

F. imperialis sulpherino

capsules and lodge on the soil surface to be covered by loose matter and kept viable until conditions favour germination, or to begin germinating quickly if those conditions already prevail.

Nevertheless, seed retains its viability for a reasonable length of time provided it is kept in correct storage conditions; in the absence of specialized facilities like those used for banks of seed held by organizations such as Kew Gardens or seed merchants, the main items to consider are temperature, moisture and cleanliness. Seed is usually ready for harvesting in early summer and this should be done as soon as capsules are ripe and before any spillage. If seed is to be stored, the capsules should be emptied on to a sheet of clean paper, the chaff very gently wafted away and the good seed dried for an hour or so in an airy but windless spot before being slid into a clean packet or envelope and clearly labelled. Check that the seed is free of obvious mould or fungus. Any seed that appears to be infected by the mycelium of fungus in the pod is going to be completely sabotaged, and apparently clean seed from close to any such fungus should only be kept if the seed is particularly precious; soak it in a fungicide before drying it. If the seed is to be kept for only a few days before sowing the packets can be stored in a cool dry spot. Any that is to be stored for more than a couple of weeks might be better placed on the top shelf of the refrigerator in a container that will prevent any damp getting to the seed, where it will be safe for some months. However, the ideal is to sow the seed immediately from the pod.

You should be able to harvest plenty of seed from many fritillary species, although there are a few with fertility problems – often clones within a species that are reluctant to set seed from their own pollen. By using pollen from another clone of the same species pollination may be successful. Insects such as wasps are the normal means of pollination, but a number of fritillaries will flower early before there are many insects about. In this case use a small watercolour brush to collect pollen from one flower and dust it generously over the whole stigma of the potential seed parent.

When the pods turn to dry-looking vessels you must harvest immediately as within only a few days a podful can be lost to the wind. If one pod is a little green but obviously not long behind the others, you can harvest this at the same time and place all the pods on a sheet of paper in a dry airy place to finish off ripening in safety.

As soon as seed is ready to be shed, the whole lot can be sown. The fresher the seed the better the germination, and this can be achieved either in a greenhouse or alpine house or outside.

Only the easiest, commonest and most robust kinds (for example *F. meleagris*) can successfully be sown outside where the plants are needed. Seed is most easily managed in pots or pans, 15cm (6 inch) diameter ones being probably the smallest practicable. Use compost consisting of approximately equal parts of coarse sand or grit, loam or healthy garden soil and peat. This gives a grittier compost than the standard John Innes seed compost, which is made of two parts of loam to one of sand and one of peat. However, the John Innes compost does have the advantage of containing added nutrients and sterilized loam which will prevent most pests and diseases attacking the seed and young seedlings, so using this compost with some added grit is a good solution.

F. meleagris 'Artemis' is one of the best-marked of the named clones of this popular European species, with a pervasive greyish sheen.

Sow the seed thinly and cover it with up to 5mm (¼ inch) of grit, coarse sand or Perlite. Keep the pots in a greenhouse, alpine house or bulb frame where you can make sure that they neither dry out nor become water-logged; to this end, stand them on capillary matting or plunge them in peat, sand or grit and keep it moist. Cover the pots with polythene or similar material until germination takes place and keep them out of direct sunlight. Seedlings normally appear through the soil at roughly the same time as the parent bulbs come into growth.

It is wise to leave the seedlings in pots for two full growing seasons before planting them out into their permanent quarters. Occasionally they will bloom in three years if treated in the same manner as mature bulbs, but they will usually need to be grown a further two years outside before they produce flowers and some kinds can take longer.

When turning pots of seedlings out, take care of all the contents. If you start looking from the top of the soil you may begin to become despondent; you may well hit gold lower down, even among the crocks at the very bottom of the pot. The majority of fritillary bulbs have a habit of pulling themselves almost as low as they are able to in pots.

BULBLETS

The procedure for propagating with bulblets is not dissimilar to that used with seed. The smaller they are the easier it is to grow them on in pots, though some of the easier species can be propagated outside with no difficulty; *F. acmopetala* and *F. uva-vulpis* grown in the garden can produce ten or more bulblets in a season. The more shallowly the bulblets are planted the more their energy gets diverted into bulb rather than flower production, so take care to plant them deeply or they will start into the vegetative cycle of reproduction before producing flowers.

Left to their own devices in ground that they find acceptable, some species will produce good clumps after two or three years. In Britain, such amenable kinds include most of the European species as well as prolific Asian species such as *F. pallidiflora*. If you leave them too long they can become overcrowded, in which case lift them as soon as the foliage and stems have faded and seedpods are ripe enough to harvest. Carefully remove the whole clump to a plastic garden tidy, a sheet of poly-

These are typical flowers of *F. uva-vulpis*, a species from Turkey and Asia Minor that will naturalize easily in the UK.

thene or something similar where the bulbs can be sorted out. The larger ones can be replanted immediately in the flowering positions, but with a little more space; some of the bulblets can accompany these groups. These small bulbs will then be safely located. If you have plenty of them it may be sensible to grow some on in a nursery row for a season or so. Some of the more precious ones can be planted up in the bulb frame or even in pots.

The American species with their easily detachable rice grain bulblets need handling with care both when lifting and sorting from the soil and when keeping in store, as the little bulblets are soon lost. They can be shaken or brushed off and sown like seed in pots with a rather deeper layer of grit over them. If this is done in the summer or autumn, you may expect to see the first thin leaves in the new year. These young plants will normally grow on to produce flowering-sized plants a

F. liliacea from California is one of the loveliest of all fritillaries for growing in a pot.

have only two scales, but they do vary and some, for example *Fritillaria liliacea*, are closer to lily structure than others. As the bulbs do not have many scales, to avoid completely destroying them it is best to detach only one of the few thick fleshy scales of this species or most other non-American species. Soak the scales for 15–20 minutes in a solution of systemic fungicide, then enclose them in damp vermiculite in a labelled plastic bag and keep them warm but not hot, around 18–21°C (65–70°F), for a period of a few weeks. Within 6–8 weeks small bulblets should have appeared at the base of the scales. These, together with their attendant scales, can then be potted up in normal fritillary potting mix (see page 35). Alternatively, the scales can be inserted in a gritty compost in pots with the top of the scale either just proud of the surface or just below. Plunge the pots into trays filled with peat or sand so that they are kept just moist. Again, bulblets should form within 6–8 weeks.

The large bulbs of *F. persica* are usually composed of two tightly clasped scales. It is normally impossible to detach a complete scale, and this also goes for other species with tight bulbs. However, a reasonable portion of such a scale will produce bulblets at the base. (Do not forget to soak the damaged parent bulb in systemic fungicide before replanting it.)

FEEDING SMALL PLANTS

Plants grow at a faster pace now than at any other time in their life and giving plenty of attention to their care will be repaid by earlier flowering. This is the time to save a year! Make sure that they are not waterlogged, and once the leaves are unfurled apply a little dilute tomato fertilizer. This will be high in potash, which tends to suit all bulbs and certainly appears to improve their general health. Applications of foliar feed used with a wetting agent can help to move things forward. Try two or three applications, the first one at half strength.

season quicker than plants raised from seed sown at the same time. Nevertheless, the waiting period can be three, four or five years.

Perhaps the bulb frame is one of the best places to grow on seedlings or bulblets. Once planted they can be left severely alone and you need not worry about the soil becoming compacted as this mirrors natural conditions. All you need do is to allow water in the growing period (but not in excess even then), to dry off thoroughly during the summer and only disturb the soil as much as is needed to remove any weeds.

SCALES

This procedure follows the same pattern as that used for lilies. Few fritillaries have scales as numerous as the most modest of lilies such as *Lilium concolor* and many

BREEDING

Up to now gardeners have done relatively little crossbreeding of fritillaries. In the wild there are species that grow together and occasionally cross-pollinate to give viable seed and resultant hybrids. Normally these are fairly closely related species, so the hybrid offspring are not hugely different from their parents. The

PLATE VIII
All flowers shown at
approximately ½ size

gardener has to be very sure when starting a breeding programme that there is a strong case for raising and introducing hybrid progeny, as it would be a shame to lose the distinction of the species under a welter of hybrids that offer little more than the species themselves. On the other hand it is highly likely that a range of hybrids could be bred from most species that would perform in the garden better than the wild plants; most gardeners would feel that this was a big gain. Some alpine purists may think this is wrong, but many grow quite a number of hybrids in their alpine collections and even if they do refuse to hybridize they are always on the lookout for improved forms and conduct a rigorous programme of selection among their seedlings. This is not far removed from a programme of hybridization.

At present hybrids are far from easy to find and the best bet is to try your own breeding programme. This could be just one cross or a series, depending on time and space – mostly the former, as this is certainly no overnight venture.

The mechanics are simple. As the flowers open, remove the anthers of a potential seed parent before pollen is spilt, using small tweezers. Take pollen from the male parent by taking a split anther with tweezers and dusting the stigma of the seed parent liberally. Alternatively, a small camelhair watercolour brush can be used to transfer pollen from the male to the female parent. It may be 3–5 days after the flowers open before pollen is readily available.

To prevent pollination by insects, enclose a de-anthered seed parent in a small paper bag if the stigma is not ripe enough to take the pollen readily – a slightly moist and tacky state. It is also a good idea to enclose the flower after pollinating it in order to prevent contamination by foreign pollen or by insects. It is essential to label each pollinated flower carefully with the name of the seed and pollen parent, the convention being that the seed parent is named first. By no means all pollinated pods will set seed – the 'take' may be very low, especially if you are crossing species of widely differing sorts. It is certainly worth increasing your chances by pollinating several flowers with the same cross; you are unlikely to get too much seed. Harvest the seed when ripe, sow immediately (see pages 48–9) and tend the seedlings until they flower in four or five years' time.

Some successful crosses include the following:

F. acmopetala × *F. latakiensis*: Natural hybrids which produce flowers similar to *F. acmopetala* with dark brown and purple bells on tall stems.

F. bithynica carica × *F. pinardii*: Natural hybrids with intermediate flowers.

F. conica rixii × *F. euboeica*:Delightful dwarf plants with small yellow flowers.

F. imperialis × *F. raddeana*: Robust plants with primrose-yellow flowers; the blossom of *F. raddeana* on the stout stems of *F. imperialis*.

F. latifolia aurea × *F. pinardii*: These hybrids look like neither parent, with recurved, conical bells with deeply pitted nectaries, each petal golden-yellow chequered green and brown.

F. michailovskyi × *F. crassifolia kurdica*: Bulbs of this naturally occurring hybrid have been brought into cultivation from populations in Turkey. The flowers are greenish-brown, rather similar to those of *F. c. kurdica*, on short stems.

F. pontica × *F. graeca*: Light green flowers with a richer green stripe, recurving at the tips and with a reddish margin. The stems are about 15 cm (6 inches) high.

F. recurva × *F. affinis*: The petals are strongly recurved like those of *F. recurva* but the flower colour is closer to that of *F. affinis* – green, brown and yellow with some red splashes from the blood of *F. recurva*.

F striata × *F. pluriflora*: Three to five sweetly scented large pink flowers, recurving at the petal tips.

F. pinardii, which can be crossed with *F. latifolia aurea* to produce a hybrid that looks like neither parent.

6

FRITILLARIES
IN THE WILD

Most members of the *Liliaceae* family tend to bloom in summer rather than spring, but fritillaries are adapted to habitats where it is necessary to get all growth, flower and seed production completed before the onset of long dry summers. Often their homes are on mountainsides or rather arid uplands. Few are found in deep shade; such shade as they do experience is likely to be that of thin woodland, but they are more likely to be growing in locations that are sunny, with high light intensity.

Rain can be absent for months through the summer, and any other moisture underground such as that from melting snow is likely to be very scarce during this period. Many high mountain species will be buried beneath a thick blanket of snow through the winter and

F. bithynica carica, photographed in its native habitat of Fethiya, Turkey. *F. bithynica* is itself a confusing species with many variations.

so be shielded from sodden conditions during those months. It is not the sort of climate that is experienced in gardens in the UK and similar temperate regions.

Wild sites can be classified into four simplified categories:

1 Screes or scree-like rocky conditions with very free drainage and summer drought;

2 Well-drained grassy mountain slopes but with a degree of summer moisture;

3 Clay grasslands that bake almost brick-hard after flowering time;

4 Light woodland conditions with a build-up of leafmould over rocky ground which is dry for months in the summer.

As a generalization, many of the Turkish and Asian species will belong in the first category of conditions, while European species tend to fall into the second. A substantial number of the Americans live in the third category, while the fourth category overlaps some of the others and accounts for the habitats of nearly half of the species.

Many species are relatively scarce in the wild, and some which were once found in large numbers have been hugely reduced by the advance of agriculture, over-grazing and the development of land for dwellings and other activities. A few have been found sufficiently pro-lific in the past to be used for feed and alleged medical benefits and one or two species are cultivated for these purposes in the East. Fritillaries are not normally very good for eating and are poisonous when raw. A few kinds

F. davisii has proved one of the most rewarding species in cultivation, increasing very rapidly.

are propagated as a cash crop, including *F. pallidiflora*, which is considered to have medicinal properties.

HABITATS

The most important factors in habitats are soil types, temperatures through the different seasons, the supply of water and the associated community of plants. As far as fritillaries are concerned the number of grazing ani-mals and the extent of human exploitation of the plants

Plants of *F. persica* growing in a typical habitat in the area between Aydincik and Gulnar in southern Turkey. This species is perhaps the most distinct of the genus.

and their environments threaten the survival of several species now and in the moderately near future.

One of the species with a wide distribution is *F. meleagris* (snake's head fritillary). This is found in a few sites in the UK and through Northern Europe across to the Caucasus Mountains. It is most often found in grassland, both grazed pastures and meadow areas kept for hay. It is soon lost from ground that is ploughed. Typical habitats are wet meadows that are flooded or at least very wet in the winter but become progressively drier through spring and summer. It appears to be more often found on neutral to slightly acid soils. In garden conditions plants can flourish near the base of a not too dominant deciduous tree, in very light woodland conditions

or in thin rather than coarse grass. Like other species grown in grass, they are lost in it when not in conspicuous flower or holding ripe seed pods.

Rather similar to *F. meleagris* in flower and habit is *F. involucrata* from the French and Italian rivieras, growing often at altitudes of 1,000m (3,500ft) in the Maritime Alps. It perhaps looks more dainty and truly in peasant character found growing here rather than in the garden, where it takes almost too readily to the soft life, growing more freely and producing greater numbers of blooms held on considerably taller stems. However, if you need only one plant of this appearance the better-known snake's head fritillary is cheaper and easier to purchase.

Also found in western Europe is the distinctive *F. pyrenaica*. Not very long ago it was regarded a relatively familiar species in south-eastern France and northern Spain, but it is now less common. It grows on dry mountainsides with grasses and other alpine plants as company. It has been known to have escaped from British gardens into the countryside. Also in northern Spain and Portugal is *F. lusitanica*, found in thin pine forests and juniper scrub on rocky poor soils at heights of around 1,500–2,000m (5,000–6,500ft). Bulbs brought into cultivation grow easily enough in gritty well-drained soil in fully exposed spots.

F. meleagroides, found in Bulgaria, and through to Moldavia, the Ukraine and parts of Asia, grows in sites not dissimilar to those of *F. meleagris*. Other species found in Bulgaria and former Yugoslavia include a clutch that live on rocky limestone: *F. drenovskyi* at 1,200–1,800m (4,000–6,000ft) in Bulgaria, *F. pontica* from sparsely wooded hillsides in Bulgaria and also in Asia Minor where it seems to enjoy some shade and gritty soils, and the still rarer *F. stribrnyi* from arid, hot slopes of sandy soil in southern Bulgaria. Further south, in Greece, there are a number of species, the most widely distributed being *F. graeca*, which is usually found on stony slopes and screes but sometimes in sparse pine woods at 120–2,400m (400–8,000ft). *F. conica*, *F. davisii* and *F. ionica* are found on rocky limestone, while the rare *F. ehrhartii* grows in non-calcareous but still gritty schist-type soils in the Greek island group the Cyclades.

F. crassifolia is a very variable plant and stands in the centre of a complex of related species. It is widely available and is very popular as it increases rapidly and is one of the easiest fritillaries to grow.

F. assyriaca, an easy species that often has a yellow tip to each petal. The nectary of this species exudes a pungent, foxy aroma, but it is most distinctive for its strong grey-green leaves. However, it is often confused with *F. uva-vulpis*.

In the garden they seem to be perfectly happy with a drained sunny site of gritty loam with some leafmould, this last ingredient seemingly especially enjoyed by *F. rhodokanakis*, which comes from the same part of the world, growing in rocky ground on limestone hills.

EASTERN MEDITERRANEAN BASIN, TURKEY & ASIA MINOR

In Turkey, the Lebanon, Syria, Iran and adjoining countries the summers are hotter and drier. Here the fritillaries often grow in highish altitudes where

temperatures can be very high during the day but drop dramatically at night. One of the more accommodating of species under cultivation is *F. acmopetala*, which is found growing in Cyprus and widely through Asia Minor including Syria. It grows from sea level to some 1,200m (4,000ft) and is found in light woodland on limestone ranges but more frequently in the stony ground of arable fields. It is regarded as a weed here, with plants able to reproduce quickly, making perhaps 8–12 bulblets each season. This liberal propagation can be invasive in gardens too, where it produces lots of bulbs of below flowering size. The answer is to plant deeply in gritty soil with a covering of at least 10cm (4 inches). It is happy to grow up through light shrubby support such as is given by the less dense lavenders, potentillas, brooms or cistus bushes. *F. elwesii* is found in Asia Minor and grows wild in scrubby conditions; it is close to *F. acmopetala* botanically as well as in habitat.

F. caucasica of hort., correctly *F. armena caucasica*, comes from the Caucasus, where it is to be found growing on the higher grassy slopes. *F. armena* is a close relative, rather more dwarf, and is found in Turkey on the dry higher areas around Ankara, growing on steep slopes with the minimal vegetation to be found in these arid areas. It also grows on limestone screes and high ground in southern Asia Minor. Most of these plants growing in open arid conditions are likely to establish themselves more successfully in hollows or to the lee of a rock or clump of vegetation.

ASIA

Widely scattered through the Lebanon and across into Iraq, *F. crassifolia* is a variable plant in its adaption to its habitats, in more open areas being only half or a third of the height it can achieve near the shelter of substantial limestone bluffs or cliffs. *F. persica* is found in Asia Minor, particularly in Iran, while *F. bithynica* belongs to the western parts of Asia Minor on high ground in lightly wooded sandy regions. Also from Iraq is *F. assyriaca*, growing in fields and hillsides around 1,500–1,800m (5,000–6,000ft) where deeper soil has collected and where there may be more moist conditions.

F. raddeana is one of the few close relatives of the well-known crown imperial *F. imperialis*. It is widespread in the wild and is said to be easy to grow in the open garden, but is rarely offered for sale.

F. imperialis is distributed throughout Iran and spreads from there to Afghanistan and northern India. It grows in a variety of sites, possibly in high treeless rocky mountain slopes, but also in shaded crevices and ravines with more plentiful moisture.

F. cirrhosa ranges from Nepal and the Himalayas through into China, growing in screes and acid soils in juniper and other scrub, a moist habitat for its growing time but drying out for a long period before the monsoon rains. In Kashmir *F. c. roylei* is to be found in high grazing land and forest clearances, growing in non-limestone areas at heights of around 3,300–3,600m (11,000–12,000ft).

F. karadaghensis, *F. raddeana* and *F. karelinii* are native to Iran, with the latter also spreading widely over Afghanistan and Turkestan, growing well at altitudes of 1,800–2,700m (6,000–9,000ft) in hot dry sites. *F. raddeana* is more restricted to the north of Iran and Turkestan, where it grows on calcareous soils. The unusual *F. sewerzowii* grows in Turkestan and other parts of central Asia, at heights of 900–1,800m (3,000–6,000ft).

Only a hardy plant will grow in Siberia at altitudes around 2,700m (9,000ft), and *F. pallidiflora* is certainly this. It is to be found in various areas of central Asia and in some parts is grown in ridges like potatoes, the bulbs being sold in markets for their possible medicinal properties. It does well in British gardens, which are lush by comparison, seeding freely and being one of the easiest and quickest to raise from seed, blooming the third year after sowing.

NORTH AMERICA

Half of the interesting American species are to be found in the Great Valley of California. Even more obviously than in other parts of the globe, most species have very prescribed limits to their distribution, some being apparently confined to an area of a few kilometres. They have their preferred habitats, half appearing to enjoy partial shade or growing in rocky soils in bright sunlight but close to the cooling sea. Alternatively, they will be growing on dry slopes below pines. The other half grow in uninterrupted sunshine in soils that may be loamy or formed from soft rocks with a high sandy magnesium silicate content, though most grow in clay adobe soils that can become baked hard as bricks for months after the spring. However, *F. affinis* and its forms can be found growing in moist, well-shaded but still open areas where the stems will be tall, and are also in dry open spots facing the sun when they will be perhaps less than half the height.

In California and Oregon *F. pluriflora* grows in adobe soils in the lower hills up to 50–450m (175–1,500ft), while *F. striata* is found on similar soils but at heights up to 750m (2,500ft). In the lower fields of the Great Valley *F. agrestis* is one of the more widely scattered species, though its range does not compare with such kinds as *F. atropurpurea*, which spreads from California and Oregon down to New Mexico and across to Idaho, the Dakotas, Nevada and Nebraska. *F. pudica* belongs to wide stretches of the western parts of the USA and into British Columbia. *F. brandegeei* grows around the pine forests at 1,500–2,100m (5,000–7,000ft) in California on granite hills.

To the north-west of California and south-west of Oregon, *F. glauca* grows at around 600–2,100m (2,000–7,000ft) on crumbly sandy rock soils, while *F. purdyi* is found restricted to the inner coastal ranges of California at similar elevation. The latter species may overlap some of the distribution of *F. recurva*, but the latter is found also in southern Oregon and western Nevada.

The odd plant out is *F. camschatcensis*, which grows from Washington State across to the coast, up through the Canadian Pacific borders to Alaska and then reappears in Japan. It seems that it was here when the land-masses were joined and that some of the territory it now occupies was regained after the last ice ages but that it has successfully moved further southwards in Asia and North America in fresh colonization. It may even colonize a British garden, as it is one of the easier kinds in a soil enriched with leafmould, perhaps with some light shade and with more moisture than is usual for orthodox species.

The rare *F. pluriflora* is a glorious plant but not easy to grow, even in an alpine house or greenhouse. Unfortunately it is also becoming rare in its wild habitat of grazing land of the Sierra Nevada, California.

7
PEOPLE & THEIR PLANTS

Some of the most knowledgeable fritillary growers in Britain have kindly agreed to share their experience in this book. Their generosity with time and expertise is another reflection of the great goodwill among gardeners and fritillary growers in particular. There is no fritillary society or special interest group at present, but fanciers are to be found in the Alpine Garden Society and the Lily group of the Royal Horticultural Society. There are of course many other dedicated growers and knowledgeable plantspeople, but with space at a premium just a few were invited to contribute.

KATH DRYDEN

Mrs Kath Dryden has long been one of our most respected growers of alpines and bulbous plants. She has served in many capacities in the Alpine Garden Society and is a well-known figure to very many enthusiasts; her experience and judgement are valued by all who know her and certainly not least by fritillary growers. Kath warns that no one can succeed with all species – many will always be tricky and it serves the genus ill if too much is claimed for it as popular plants. These are bulbs for the dedicated grower.

'Many people grow good garden fritillaries such as *F. imperialis* and *F. meleagris*, and then go on to experiment with different kinds from places further afield, such as *F. pyrenaica*, *F. graeca*, *F. lusitanica* and *F. camschatcensis*, with varying degrees of success. They become intrigued by a fascinating genus, and try to cultivate more and more species.

'A great many have to be grown in bulb frames, beds under glass or pots. These are regularly shown in competitive classes of specialist societies. The vast majority are bone hardy as far as cold is concerned. Some species

such as *F. bucharica*, *F. stenanthera* and *F. gibbosa* come from the old USSR and Turkey. Others, such as *F. rixii*, *F. euboeica* and *F. rhodokanakis* hail from Greece and neighbouring countries and of course the Aegean islands. By far the most species grow naturally in Turkey. In such climates they have very warm long summers of rest, but not in the baking heat that is so often suggested – in the wild they often grow at great depths and are so insulated from the worst of the summer's heat.

'There are also species which grow in the eastern states of America from southern California to Canada and Alaska. Here we can find an enormous range of climates and temperatures. On the coastal range of California occur the tender sorts such as *F. biflora* and *F. liliacea*. These really do need frost-free conditions.

'Many others such as *F. recurva* have evolved and adapted to woodland conditions. One might assume that it and other American woodland kinds would find British woodland conditions to their liking. Sadly they do not. However the widespread *F. affinis* can be coaxed and provided the woodland is not artificially watered during the summer, it will do well enough.

'Others from California and Oregon are true alpine mountain dwellers and as such should be given alpine treatment plus a dryish and cool summer rest. Some water percolates the rocky terrain in the form of dew, so all is not bone dry. Here the top growth dies down much later and in the garden they should be allowed to rest well into the autumn season.

'The growing of specialist fritillaries can give one at the same time both endless frustration and endless pleasure. To flower a tricky bulb 7–10 years after sowing the seed equals euphoria!

F. recurva is one of the most distinct and attractive of the American species, and the only one that is red. It is not a rampant grower in cultivation.

'The term 'frost-free' immediately rings alarm bells for some as it implies expensive installation and running costs. These gardeners do not stop to think that the domestic refrigerator is frost-free at a steady 2–4°C (36–39°F), a contrast to our winter climate which regularly swings from intense wet cold to several degrees above zero and back again. After each thaw the plants may begin a new burst of growth only for the return of bitter cold to give another check, the cause of many losses. We need to supply conditions closer to those of our refrigerators. The same frame lights that kept off the summer rains can be replaced after arranging layers of bubble plastic and fleece which will help to even out the fluctuations of temperature. Pots plunged up to their rims at all times will be kept in more equable conditions, whether plastic or clay.

'It is much easier to over-dry the bulbs in summer in plastic pots; they get much hotter than clays. Also these plastic ones only have direct interaction with their environment through their top soil surface and the drainage holes, a contrast to clays which are interactive on all surfaces. Successful growers trickle water between clay pots plunged in sand about once a month during the long rest period.

'To maintain fritillaries in health year after year give them a good steady food supply in the shape of a loam-based compost. Woodland species like extra humus as leafmould or a very finely shredded bark.'

DR CHRIS GREY-WILSON

Dr Chris Grey-Wilson is well-known to members of the Alpine Garden Society, of which he has long been a leading member. He is one of the foremost plant explorers of the present day and as such has much of interest to say about some of the fritillaries he has found growing in the wild.

Fritillaria delavayi

'Little was known of this species until its rediscovery in north-western Yunnan in June 1987 by the Sino-

British Lijiang Expedition (SBLE). Ron McBeath and I were traversing a steep scree at about 3,800m (12,500ft) above the Snow Pine Village, Yulong Shan, north of Lijiang. It was the end of of long day and we were on our way back down the mountain. Among the rocks we suddenly came upon several plants of *F. delavayi*. This is a very distinct species bearing a large grey-brown bell with a purplish flush on the exterior. Flowering plants have several broad oblong, somewhat recurved, grey-green leaves. This is undoubtedly a scarce and local species; I have not seen it elsewhere, although it is known to occur in Bhutan and presumably at localities in between. An interesting feature of the species is the way the tepals persist in fruit, surrounding it in a papery envelope. The purpose of this is not clear but it is assumed that the tepals aid seed distribution – the whole head breaks away and is blown across the scree scattering seeds as it goes. The species is confined to scree habitats.'

Fritillaria cirrhosa

'This species is common in the mountains of western China, where I have seen it on numerous occasions. It is immensely variable from one area to another. Chinese botanists believe that these variations represent a series of closely related species and as a result they have described a number of new species in recent years.

'In the Gang-ho-ba (Yulong Shan) *F. cirrhosa* is locally common on grassy valley gravels at about 3,000m (10,000ft). Plants grow to about 25cm (10 inches) and have pairs of leaves, the uppermost in a whorl of three with scarcely any coiled tip. The flowers are solitary or occasionally paired. They are bell-shaped, not flared, green with purplish-brown tessellations. Sometimes the whole flower can be dark with hardly noticeable tessellations, while others may be greenish-yellow without obvious, or just a few, tessellations.

'At Tianchi Lake fritillaries said also to be *F. cirrhosa* can be found growing on rhododendron moorland at 4,000m (13,200ft); most actually grow in the shrubs. These plants are far taller, 50–60cm (20–24 inches), the upper leaves with twining and clinging tips. The flowers are more elegant flared bells, greenish-yellow or purplish-brown, generally with mild tessellation.

'I have also seen the species in Nepal on a number of occasions, most notably in the Marsyandi valley at

F. stenanthera is a tiny plant in its natural habitat, but in gardens can be more than twice its wild height.

about 4,300m (14,000ft), growing on steep slopes among low rhododendrons. The plants were generally stouter than the Chinese plants and the flowers both broader and squarer but with similar coloration. The overall appearance is closer perhaps to *F. c. roylei*. It is often found in this valley with *Lilium nanum*.'

Fritillaria unibracteata

'This species is known only from western Sichuan, where I have seen it on the Balang Shan, west of Chengdu, at about 4,300m (14,000ft). Here it grows in sloping alpine meadows together with *Cypripedium tibeticum*, *Omphalogramma vinciflora* and other exciting plants. *F. unibracteata* is readily distinguished by having alternate leaves and rather small solitary flowers, greenish-yellow or reddish-purple, without obvious tessellations.'

Fritillaria imperialis

'I saw this on several occasions in Afghanistan in 1971, sometimes in large colonies but always in the typical deep orange-red colour. Interestingly, nearly all the plants I saw in the wild were growing in rock crevices, possibly the only safe spots in a heavily grazed region. The best colonies were to the north-west of Ghazni, south-west of Kabul in the southern Hindu Kush.'

Fritillaria bucharica

'This well-known species is common at the higher altitudes in the Amankhutan valley near Samarkand in Kazakhstan, where I have seen it in full flower in April. It is found in rocky places, flowering soon after the snow has melted and growing in association with plants like *Corydalis ledbouriana*, *Crocus korolkowii*, *Iris warleyensis*, *Colchicum kesselringii* and a host of other interesting bulbs. Plants show little variability except in size, though this is probably due to age and bulb size. The dense racemes of white flowers nod at the tip. It is usually found in very rocky places on mountain slopes.'

Fritillaria stenanthera

'I have only seen this growing in the Chimgan valley near Tashkent, in April. This valley is a haven for bulbous plants which flower in profusion soon after the snow has gone: *Tulipa kaufmanniana*, *T. butlovii*, *T. turkestanica*, *T. chimganica*, *Colchicum luteum* and *Korolkowia sewerzowii* (included in this volume under the name *Fritillaria sewerzowii*).

'*F. stenanthera* is a small plant in this valley, rarely more than 7cm (2¾ inches) tall and with just 2–3 flowers. In cultivation the same plants are far more vigorous with many more flowers to the raceme. In the Chimgan valley it grows on rocky slopes, and only rarely on the valley floor.'

Fritillaria pyrenaica var. lutea

'*F. pyrenaica*, the type species, is common in parts of the Pyrenees, especially around Gavarnie in the French Pyrenees. The majority of plants are the normal colour, rarely as dark as some forms seen in cultivation. However, on one occasion I stopped just north of Gavarnie to admire rich meadows full of daffodils (*Narcissus pseudonarcissus* ssp. *abscissus*). Among these I spotted a number of plants of *F. pyrenaica*, some with yellowish-green unmarked flowers. This, *F. pyrenaica*

var. *lutea*, is a rare plant in cultivation. It does not come true from seed, but if selfed yellow will appear again in the progeny in the second and third generations.'

JOHN HILL

John Hill is an enthusiastic grower of fritillaries who has converted a hobby into a nursery business which specializes in small bulbs and alpines. He grows in the West Midlands. Like most enthusiasts, John admits to always learning, and sometimes learns to reject established wisdom. He writes of his experience of the cultivation of fritillaries.

'While I try to discover as much as possible about the natural habitats, soil, aspect, altitude and climate of each species, this information can be misleading. *Fritillaria pluriflora* and some other American species grow

F. pluriflora, photographed in the Bear Valley, California. In this habitat it is vulnerable to overgrazing by cattle, which eat the flowers before they can reproduce.

wild in heavy clay. They are very unlikely to manage in such soil in the British climate. Nevertheless, a friend grows *F. camschatcensis* in a predominantly clay loam and flowers it well.

'Almost all species have a good-quality John Innes No 2 compost as the basis of the growing medium. The usual mix is three parts John Innes No 2, one part leaf-mould, three parts sharp grit and one part sharp sand. I only use peat for a very few species such as *F. camschatcensis*. Using coir in place of leaf mould was not a success, and peat-based composts seem totally unsuitable.

'Once rooting is firmly established I apply a general fertilizer to encourage strong foliage leading to good bulb development. When growth is well above ground I use a high potash fertilizer to promote flower bud formation for the following year.

'A few species such as *F. camschatcensis* and *F. meleagris* are grown in a peat bed, the former in lattice pots where the partial root restriction seems to encourage flowering. A number of more robust kinds grow in the rock garden, in particular *F. pontica* and *F. acmopetala* – both accidental arrivals via the old bulb compost used when constructing alpine beds. A wider range of species are reasonably successful in beds made specially for

F. pudica makes an engaging pot plant but can also be grown outside in a trough garden or scree.

bulbs. Raised beds approximately 23–30cm (9–12 inches) high around small trees are used for species such as *F. acmopetala*, *F. involucrata*, *F. pontica*, *F. pyrenaica* and *F. uva-vulpis*. They are planted on the sunniest side and the trees help to reduce moisture during the dormant season. These kinds maintain themselves and tend to increase steadily by bulb division.

'Three years ago some new beds were made incorporating old bulb compost. Rice grains from some American species were accidentally introduced. Now *F. affinis* and its form *F. a. tristulis* are established flowering plants. I am experimenting with rice grains from *F. pudica* and the form *F. pudica* 'Seattle Giant'. This may be an easier method of growing on bulbs than under protection, where their propensity to fall apart when handling causes difficulties.'

POT CULTIVATION

'After several years of using clay pots for protected cultivation, I have now changed over to lattice pots plunged into gritty compost – not sand. They do not completely dry out and roots can travel out of the pots. The pots can be easily lifted and dropped into larger clays for exhibition. The smallest practical size of lattice pot is 8cm (3 ½ inches) diameter, available from orchid stockists. Lifting one of these pots that has become overful can cause a check to bulb development for the following season.

'Three different sites are used for beds: a raised bed covered by Dutch lights in extreme weather, a raised bed covered with an Access frame and a bulb bed within the alpine house.

'Stock plants of the more vigorous kinds such as *F. acmopetala*, *F. pallidiflora*, *F. pyrenaica* and *F. uva-vulpis* are housed in the first with concrete block sides and only covered with the lights in very wet winter or summer weather. Ventilation remains open at all times. This bed is also used for high-altitude species which do not want undue drying out in summer: *F. armena*, *F. a. caucasica*, *F. latifolia*, *F. michailovskyi*, *F. minuta*, *F. reuteri* and *F. tubiformis*. After failing with *F. alburyana* in the two more protected beds, I find it succeeds in the harder conditions and flowers at its normal height, not at or even below soil level!

'The Access frame is used for more delicate lower-level Mediterranean plants, including the fritillaries. The 1.2m (4ft) wide frame allows easy opening to suit

F. michailovskyi is now widely available, a triumph of microropagation, and is an easy plant to grow. Recently plants have appeared carrying up to seven blooms on a stem.

different species and is adjusted according to the weather. Lattice pots are plunged into gritty compost and the whole is kept moist during the growing season. Sliding side vents are kept open and top panes removed in early spring. Several kinds will elongate if kept covered too long once they show through the surface. In this bed I grow *F. carica, F. conica, F. davisii, F. drenovskyi, F. ehrhartii, F. sewerzowii* and others. The top glass panes are replaced once top growth has died down. As none of these species appreciate baking the frame is shaded in hot weather.

'The alpine house bulb bed is divided into two. Both sections have gritty compost but one section is limy and the other completely lime-free. The lime part is used for the Rhinopetalum section species, *F. bucharica, F. gibbosa, F. karelinii* and *F. stenanthera*. For these the compost consists of equal parts of John Innes No 2 compost and sharp grit. All are kept dormant until late autumn,

so reducing the likelihood of flowers at ground level. The lime-free part is used for the American species which are again repotted later than normal. These include *F. affinis, F. a. tristulis, F. a.* 'Wayne Roderick', *F. atropurpurea, F. glauca, F. pluriflora, F. pudica* and *F. recurva*. Apart from top-dressing, the rice grain species are left undisturbed for at least two years to avoid fragile bulbs disintegrating.

'Apart from the Rhinopetalum and American species, repotting of most is carried out by the end of the summer. The pots are emptied in midsummer and the bulbs stored in paper bags in a cool place for a few weeks – not polythene bags, as condensation can encourage botrytis. Moisture-loving species such as *F. camschatcensis* are stored in moist peat but if possible are repotted immediately.

'Some species such as *F. acmopetala* and *F. minuta* tend to make many small bulbs at the expense of flowering potential. It helps to plant these kinds deeply and to keep them cool.'

PROPAGATION

'Propagation is tackled as seems fit for the species. A few have bulbs that divide quickly, making it easy to get a potful of identical plants. However, some are stubborn and a decade can pass with little happening! Home-collected seed is sown in the autumn using 3 parts John Innes No 1, 1 part vermiculite and 2 parts sharp grit. All seed pots are exposed to the weather until germination starts, when they are brought into the alpine house. The pots are then left undisturbed for at least two years. They are fed with half-strength tomato fertilizer and certainly never dried out when dormant.

'Seed from elsewhere often arrives in the New Year; it may not germinate until the following winter and frequently germination is less free than with fresh seed. The seed from botanic gardens or professional collectors is more reliably named than that distributed by various societies; as it may take 3–6 years to flower these new plants it is helpful to have the correct name on the label. Most difficult are the Rhinopetalums; germination can be good but getting moisture content right after they die down for their first season is critical – too much and they rot, too little and they shrivel. Another difficulty arises from the self-sterility of several cultivated clones. One needs to get another clone of the species to cross pollinate – or to beg pollen of another clone.'

8
FRITILLARIES
IN NORTH AMERICA

The number of American *Fritillaria* species is around 19, the exact figure depending on the botanist one follows and the status given to certain plants. All the native American species as well as those of other continents are regarded as quality plants by most gardeners in the United States, especially those who are particularly interested in wild species and smaller plants. American gardeners find that their native species need to be cultivated as carefully as in Europe or elsewhere. The different climatic zones afford varied conditions for the plants, some favouring certain species, but on the whole the species found to be easy in the Old World are easy in the New and, likewise, the difficult are as tricky.

The North American species include some outstanding plants that are gorgeous in bloom, although there are one or two strange species such as the maverick *F. brandegeei*, with its seemingly ill-kempt starry flowers. The first thing that will strike the newcomer is the wide colour palette, a range from the popular pinky reds to whites, greens, yellows, browns and blacks, as well as many multicoloured forms. All are enthusiastically collected and grown in America and Europe, and they have been extensively studied and written about by leading bulb authorities. Carl Purdy, working in the USA through the 1930s, is a revered name among bulb fanciers and he did detailed work on fritillaries. D. F. Beetle's *Monograph of the North American species of Fritillaria*, published in 1944, is still a most useful production. Also in America, Wayne Roderick has for 30 years

dedicated much of his life to bulbs and to fritillaries in particular. More recently, Dr Sylvia Martinelli has published detailed results of work on the American fritillaries, and Roger McFarlane of Edinburgh Botanic Garden has also published careful descriptions and evaluations of these species and hybrids.

All the plants are found growing in the north temperate region, 30–50° latitude just as in the European and Asian kinds. Most are distributed along the west coast towards the Rockies, with *F. atropurpurea* the most widely distributed, recorded in 12 states. Five species are found growing in alpine scree conditions: *F. atropurpurea*, *F. falcata*, *F. glauca*, *F. pudica* and *F. purdyi*. Six species hide in the meadow grasses, well camouflaged when out of bloom: *F. agrestis*, *F. biflora*, *F. b. grayana*, *F. liliacea*, *F. pluriflora* and *F. striata*. Eight species grow in or around the edge of mountain woodland: *F. affinis*, *F. atropurpurea pinetorum*, *F. brandegeei*, *F. camschatcensis*, *F. micrantha*, *F. phaeanthera*, *F. recurva* and *F. viridia*.

The particular feature of some of the American species is the tiny rice grains to be found on the outside of the bulbs, usually more plentifully around the base. This most unusual means of reproduction is seen in eight species, the remaining ones having scales like lilies with no rice grains or only a token attempt at the base. The rice grain species are *F. affinis*, *F. atropurpurea pinetorum*, *F. brandegeei*, *F. camschatcensis*, *F. micrantha*, *F. phaeanthera*, *F. recurva* and *F. pudica*, though the latter has a compact scale-like bulb which may have only a few rice grains.

Climatic conditions along the west side of America where the fritillaries are most numerous are not dissimilar to those of western Europe, being warm to mild for

F. biflora is the Californian species commonly known as chocolate bells, black fritillary or mission bells. Bulbs of this plant soon begin to increase very generously.

The American *F. pudica* has the common names Johnny-jump-up and little yellow bell. It is one of the most popular fritillaries with alpine specialists.

a good period of the year and periodically moist. In the south and west the conditions are closer to those of the Mediterranean, while to the north-west the winter becomes much colder and occasionally dips to −20°C (−4°F). The soil varies but is usually a stony, loamy, clay that is well drained and becomes baked dry in summer. The fritillaries share this environment with other bulbs such as the popular erythroniums and the lilies *Lilium parryi* and *L. humboldtii*.

Three species mark themselves apart from the remainder – *F. pudica*, *F. striata* and *F. pluriflora*. The yellow *F. pudica* has a distinct style, unbroken and similar to many of the European species. There is only one other American species with an unbroken style, the tall and unusual *F. brandegeei*, the standard for the group being broken trifid styles. *F. pudica* is cytologically distinct in having 13 chromosomes rather than the 12 of the remaining species. This species is one of the most widely distributed, being found throughout the Rocky

Mountains of north-west America and southern Canada. While there is plenty of variation in colour and plant height within the specific limits, *F. pudica* does not hybridize, even though it is often found growing with *F. atropurpurea* and other species.

The other two species of the distinct trio, *F. striata* and *F. pluriflora*, are closely linked but are very distinct from all other species. The two are differently coloured, *F. pluriflora* a good pink, *F. striata* white veined brown. They do not hybridize with other species and, being found in widely distant locations, the two do not have the opportunity to interbreed, something that horticulturalists have undertaken successfully. In the wild *F. pluriflora* can often be found growing with *F. affinis* and further towards the north with *F. recurva*, *F. purdyi* and *F. glauca*. *F. striata* grows with *F. brandegeei* and *F. atropurpurea pinetorum*.

One of the more clearly defined species is the black-flowered *F. camschatcensis*, which has an unusual distribution. It is found growing in woodland and moist meadows in west Alaska, north Washington State and British Columbia. However, its distribution is even wider, as it is the only American fritillary also to be found in Japan, western China and parts of the world that used to form the most eastern reaches of the USSR. It is shown on the diagram on page 72 as being at an extreme of the group but it looks close to *F. biflora* and this links it to an important group of plants.

The foliage, stems and dark flowers of *F. biflora* are similar, though the flowers are green and black; they can be seen along the west coast in grass meadows and among dwarf shrubs. This species is widespread and can be found quite freely scattered from Los Angeles to San Francisco. Where it overlaps the distribution of *F. purdyi*, a close relation, the two species will hybridize to produce the distinct plants known as *F. biflora grayana*.

F. purdyi grows mainly on very stony screes, especially where they may meet pine woodland, notably north and slightly inland from where *F. biflora* grows in the Trinity and Humboldt county. Gardeners grow a fine selected clone, *F. b.* 'Martha Roderick'.

F. liliacea is one of the most enchanting of fritillaries, graceful, white and varying only within tight limits. It is a grassland plant from around the bay of San Francisco. *F. agrestis* is a short-stemmed plant with white bells and a far wider distribution than *F. liliacea*, *F. biflora grayana* or *F. purdyi*. It is another grassland plant, found in low

F. recurva, photographed in its native habitat of Tehama County, California. In the USA this colourful species is highly attractive to humming birds.

valley lands from the bay of San Francisco down to San Luis Obispo county. It may grow with *F. biflora* but in its more inland rather than coastal locations. Other kinds that may be found growing with the above complex of plants are *F. affinis* and, less often, *F. falcata* and *F. viridia*.

The botanical position of *F. falcata* would seem to be close to *F. atropurpurea*, of which some botanists make it a varietal form. Visually there are affinities to *F. purdyi*, *F. agrestis* and *F. glauca*, but possibly the botanical links are more tentative. It is an alpine scree species to be found growing in San Benito and Santa Clara county alongside *F. biflora*, *F. agrestis*, *F. affinis* and *F. viridia*. *F. glauca* is another alpine scree plant, this time with mucky yellow flowers. It is found from Mendocino County to Oregon with others such as *F. recurva*, *F. affinis* and, much more occasionally, *F. purdyi*.

Most widespread of all the American species is *F. atropurpurea*, found in both stony screes and pine woodland that has colonized stony ground. Its brownish-red and green flowers look similar to those of *F. affinis* and *F. atropurpurea pinetorum*. It grows almost everywhere that any of the fritillaries grow; in the northern Rocky Mountains and southern part of Oregon state it may be accompanied by *F. pudica*. Towards the southern and western sections of its distribution it can occasionally be seen with *F. affinis*, *F. micrantha* and *F. recurva*.

Although *F. atropurpurea pinetorum* looks similar to *F. atropurpurea* it is also closely linked to *F. brandegeei*, which grows with *F. striata* within the *F. atropurpurea pinetorum* distribution. *F. a. pinetorum* grows to the south of *F. atropurpurea*, which is a plant of the alpine screes of the Sierra Nevada. Although *F. brandegeei* is allied to it, *F. affinis* is closer in appearance. The former species is restricted to the Kern and Tular counties where it grows in shady woodland, not the usual habitat for fritillaries.

In appearance *F. affinis* is a pivotal species with some similarities to *F. atropurpurea* and *F. brandegeei* but also with links to *F. viridia* and *F. micrantha*. It is quite alone in the *Fritillaria* genus in having so many variable diploid, triploid and tetraploid forms. It is widespread from Los Angeles to Washington state, its distribution covering coastal locations to sites 1,500m (5,000ft) high. With this spread it grows with all but a few of the other species. This multicoloured plant is usually found in wooded areas. It is surprising with its wide variation that there are not more named forms, but two well-known ones are elevated from the unnamed crowd, the delightful *F. a.* 'Wayne Roderick' and the dwarfish *F. a. tristulis*.

Two other woodland species are the similar *F. viridia* and *F. micrantha*. The first has yellowish-green flowers and has often been linked in the past with *F. affinis*. It is found growing in the Monterey and Benito counties alongside *F. affinis* and *F. agrestis*. *F. micrantha*, with yellowish-brown flowers, is distinct but has some similarities to *F. viridia* and *F. affinis*. This woodland species comes from the Sierra Nevada, where it may be found with *F. recurva*, *F. phaeanthera*, *F. atropurpurea* and occasionally *F. affinis*.

The classy species *F. recurva* has strong links with *F. micrantha*, bearing many similar features, but from the horticultural point of view it is perhaps more distinctive with a stronger recurve to the blooms. It is a variable species with a wider distribution from southern Oregon to the Nevada counties, where it may be found growing alongside *F. micrantha*. Along the western coast *F. recurva* will overlap the *F. affinis* distribution. Occasionally *F. purdyi*, *F. glauca* and *F. atropurpurea* can be seen growing with *F. recurva*, but none can rival the showiness of its shapely red blossoms. Its variation has been recognized by the naming of at least three

forms, *F. r. coccinea*, *F. r. adamantina* and *F. r. gentneri*.

Where *F. affinis* and *F. recurva* meet in the wild a series of hybrids can appear. These plants have been given no collective name, although some are to be found in cultivation. In the same way *F. micrantha* will hybridize with *F. recurva* in the Sierra Nevada but this time the resulting hybrids are gathered under the name *F. phaeanthera*. They are found in woodland situations and have flowers in a range from reddish-orange to a truer orange or a rich yellow. These plants will again interbreed with *F. recurva* to produce redder forms.

The diagrammatic chart below gives some idea of possible relationships. *F. purdyi* on one side of the chart has little in common with *F. recurva* from the other side, although they may be found growing thoroughly mixed up together. It may well be that there are several intermediate species or groups of plants that have died away in the process of evolution and some may be more successful relatively modern species. Care is needed in evaluating the status of many plants, as hybrid forms can easily be given the false respectability of specific names as in the case of *F. phaeanthera*. On the other hand it is difficult to see that *F. liliacea* is of hybrid origin, as has been suggested.

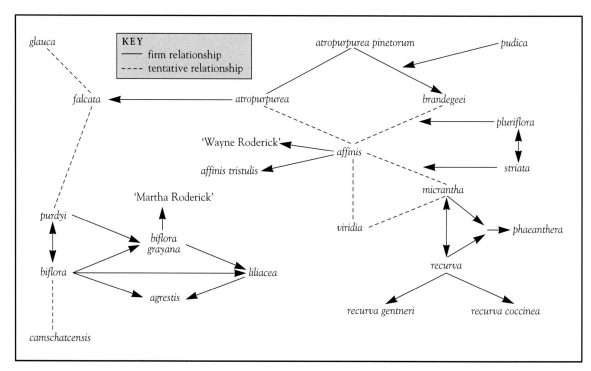

9

SHOWING FRITILLARIES

Most gardeners are introduced to the variety of the genus by seeing flowering plants at shows, for in gardens open to the public it is unusual to see more than the crown imperials and the snake's-head fritillary with perhaps an occasional *F. persica*. At spring shows alpine nurserymen may well exhibit less common species in their groups, often as highlights, and whenever the Alpine Garden Society is staging a competitive show in the spring months there will certainly be carefully grown pots of species and often specially selected forms of these species. Very few onlookers can resist their appeal, and some will succumb to the extent of becoming obsessed with competitive showing.

Showing pot-grown plants in competition is fun, and the more care you take the greater the pleasure of the rewards. These may be the first, second or third prize cards, but it is in the competition and the camaraderie of the events that the real joy is found. A novice is soon absorbed into the fraternity of fritilllary growers and given help and encouragement.

At Alpine Garden Society shows there are many classes into which fritillaries may fit, including classes for an individual pot of a bulbous plant, a collection of several pots of bulbs or a more wide collection of plant types. Fritillaries are likely to score highly in such competition, far more highly than more commonly grown and easily cultivated bulbs such as many small hybrid daffodils. (Note that while here the word 'pot' is used as most fritillaries like fairly deep soil conditions, pans with their more shallow profile are perfectly legitimate containers and may allow the competitor to house more plants together without the whole becoming too heavy and unwieldy.)

Any fritillary species has the potential to win first prize in the group of exhibits in the bulb section, but it is a fact that the judges are always more impressed by a good pot of one of the rarer or more tricky kinds. A well-grown pot of *F. gibbosa*, *F. latifolia*, *F. liliacea*, *F. pluriflora* or *F. stenanthera* will be valued very much more highly than some of the easier species, however beautiful they may be. You can study form by checking the results of previous shows published by the AGS to find the species that more often win the prizes.

PRESENTATION

Once you have picked the most show-worthy kinds, much of the likelihood of success will depend on how the plants are grown. Judges usually look for uniformity in the potful of plants, so there should be little variation in height or habit. This means there is a premium on all stock raised from a particular plant, a genetic clone. The exception to this is when the show schedule specifically quotes 'raised from seed', when some variation of habit, flower form and colour is tolerated.

Plants must be as free of blemishes from physical or fungal damage as possible. There should be no spots of dirt, damage from frost or marks caused by human handling or animal contact; even a light touch can affect those with foliage and/or flowers covered with bloom. The ideal potful will be of plants just coming to their prime, with flowers just fully opened or on the verge of being so and with some still in bud. Certainly there should be no flowers in a faded or wilted condition; should an otherwise good potful be marred by a flower that is going over, the offender should be removed cleanly, perhaps with a sharp craft knife, so that no flower stalk is left.

PLATE IX

All flowers shown
approximately full size

F. crassifolia

F. minima

F. acmopetala

F. rhodokanakis

F. elwesii

F. whittallii

F. michailovskyi Multiform, an exceptional form of an already very showy species from Turkey.

A fine entry can be spoilt by such an elementary oversight as a dirty pot. The pot should be perfect and the impression of tidiness enhanced by neat labelling. Obviously the name should be clearly written, spelt correctly and botanically exact; with fritillaries this can trip up the unwary. In your own pots at home you may have a plant labelled *F. glaucoviridis*, but on the show bench nothing less than *Fritillaria alfredae* subsp. *glaucoviridis* will do.

The top of the pot should be cleanly dressed. This may be done in a variety of ways. You may present all the pots with clean even grit or small stones, or you may just use this material or small slate pieces for the species that are recognized as normally alpine scree plants. Woodland species might have their pots top-dressed with fresh green moss, while a grassland species might look well growing from a cover of clean dark sedge peat. The top-dressing materials are a matter of personal preference, but it is of course important that the material should enhance the appearance of the plants rather than being a distraction. Pot, label and top dressing act as the framework to what ought to be a beautiful picture.

Different shows and different seasons are likely to bring changes in the judges and thus some slight differences of emphasis. There are far more classes and opportunities for showing fritillaries at the spring AGS shows than at any others. To try to formulate a list of fritillary species in order of show precedence is obviously impossible, but there are some species that most judges look kindly upon, all other matters such as cultivation and presentation being equal. A large potful of *F. latifolia aurea*, *F. davisii*, *F. hermonis amana*, *F. pinardii*, *F. pudica* or *F. purdyi* will find favour with the vast majority of alpine judges. Most importantly, these six species are small; happily they also may be expected to reproduce reasonably quickly from the original bulb, so making a pot that looks generously full.

Some of the taller species also have their place, especially in a class that requires 3–6 pots. Three will be arranged in line, with the tallest in the rear and the smallest to the front. When six are shown there will be the two tallest to the rear in the same manner and each couple should be as closely balanced in height as possible. Some of these less dwarf kinds will include species such as *F. biflora*, most clones of *F. crassifolia kurdica*, *F. involucrata*, *F. pontica* and *F. whittallii*.

GROWING WINNERS

While general pot culture has been dealt with on pages 34–5, there are points that can be made here that relate specifically to culture aimed at producing show winners. There are some species that can tolerate the fluctuating conditions in pots better than others. As a general rule, the aim is to avoid extreme and rapid changes of soil and air temperatures and of moisture content in the former. The soil should be moist to the touch during the growing season and more or less dry through the dormant summer period. One method is to plunge show pots in the garden for most of the year, bringing them indoors when the flower buds emerge through the soil. This hardy outdoor life helps to keep foliage and stems true to character without elongating them and perhaps giving a rather yellowish, anaemic look to the foliage. There are species that are early into growth and can be damaged by frost, and these certainly need bringing into alpine house conditions or into bulb frames when very inclement weather threatens.

As the first buds begin to appear on plunged pots lift the pots carefully, remove most of the soil or plunge material on the outside of the pots, and place them in a cold frame, alpine house or greenhouse. From the time of the first appearance of the buds there can easily be four or more weeks before they begin to unfurl properly, the speed depending on the weather. During this four weeks you can place the pots outside in periods of good weather, bringing them back under cover when frost is forecast. This will help to reduce the chance of stems becoming unnaturally tall. The constant handling and movement of the pots should also ensure that when the flowers open they are not all facing one way. Equally shared sunlight should ensure balanced growth and bloom.

While frost is the most obvious danger, and could overnight ruin the chances of a first prize if a good pot is left outside in very severe conditions, there are other hazards to circumvent. Slugs become more lively as the spring begins to advance; early aphids and greenhouse pests can cause problems if you have not made a good job of keeping all areas under glass as clear of pests as possible.

ORGANIZING FOR THE SHOW

The crucial time is the week before the show. You should have notified the show secretary of your entries in good time. Double check the dates – especially if you are going to several shows – and have a system of noting in a diary that you have gone through the necessary procedures. For each show, try to estimate the number of plants likely to be in bloom for the show date. With some show dates following close upon one another, a particularly good pot may be presented at several shows before the flowers fade. A certain amount of special timing may well be needed – the relative warmth of the greenhouse to bring plants forward (but without very high temperatures) and the cool of a cold frame provided with gentle shading from green netting to keep flowers from going over too quickly. Never resort to dramatic gestures such as placing a plant in the house near a sunny window, for in a few hours you could spoil all your hard work. As in all gardening matters, you will develop a feel for the needs of the plants and learn to make the most of the conditions and resources available.

Having got your plants to show pitch, take care not to let them suffer damage en route to the show bench. Anything that moves in your vehicle (including animals and children) is a danger to your plants. Before moving pots with tall stems, tie each stem loosely to a firmly implanted thin split cane, using lengths of wool or something similar. The advantage of wool is that it can be seen clearly, while nylon thread or cotton are less visible and may be caught on other objects, causing damage.

Pack the pots in carrying boxes; there are plenty of cheap, strong, plastic ones available. Within the box the pots should be wedged with newspaper, polystyrene or foam so that there is no room for movement. Then pack each box tightly in the vehicle, if need be using empty boxes to keep them firmly in place. Try to make sure that the vehicle does not get too hot and make an early start so that you can travel at modest speed and arrive with plenty of time to park, unload and take your pots into the show venue. Carry only what you can comfortably manage each time from the car to the show venue. Always double check that you have got your pots in the right class, that they are according to schedule in all particulars such as number, size of flowers and size of container, that your entry card is present and correctly filled, that no detritus has landed on the plants or pots and that labels have not become askew or misplaced. A last-minute check before the hall is cleared for the judges is always worthwhile.

Do not feel apprehensive about showing – there are beginners' classes at most shows and you will soon find other competitors with varying degrees of knowledge and experience who are willing to give advice to help you towards a first prize card bearing your name.

PLATE X

All flowers shown approximately full size

F. acmopetala

F. acmopetala

F. pontica

F. pontica

10

A–Z LIST OF FRITILLARIES

This alphabetical list has each species headed in bold type, followed by the section of the genus to which it belongs, for example 1C for the first species, *F. acmopetala*. Next is the name of the botanist who has given authority to this name by using it when publishing the first full description of the species. Names in brackets indicate the botanist giving the first full description, but the specific name may have been altered or given greater or lesser importance – for example, a specific name may have been reduced to the value of a form of another species. Also given is the form of the style of the flower, this being one of the most important diagnostic features; 'tri' is short for trifid, the style being clearly divided into three parts, 'e' is for entire, the style being without division, and 'lobed' is occasionally used when the style is intermediate with the ends being indented to make three lobes. Next is the general area where the species is found in the wild, followed by the commonly found synonyms of the species; no complete list is attempted as many will only appear in botanical literature.

Fritillaria acmopetala
(1C) Boissier, 1846: tri: Med, Asia Minor:
syn. *F. lycia, F. intermis*.
This is a rapidly increasing plant for the open garden, with a twin-scale bulb and numerous bulb offsets. The stem grows to 30–35cm (12–14 inches) with alternate, grey-green, linear leaves. At the stem base the leaves are broader; they become thinner, more scattered and more

The strong leaves of *F. acmopetala*, a plant from the Mediterranean and the Middle East which grows freely in gardens and soon makes beautiful clumps.

matt-green towards the flowers. There is 2.5–7.5cm (1–3 inches) of clear stem below the flowers. These vary in colour and number, with usually one, quite often two and sometimes three but only very rarely more. They are pendant, 3–4cm (1¼–1½ inches) long and slightly less wide, with a little constriction at the mouth before the pointed petals recurve around the tip. On the outside the basic pigment is greenish-yellow but with maroon added. Around the top there may be a band of purple and this can often extend down three-quarters of the flower. The shiny polished surface of the three inner petals is darker, a dull maroon merging with greens and yellows. The style is deeply trifid. The nectaries are deep green, raised above the surface, pitted and oblong; they emit a very unpleasant scent but one highly attractive to wasps. After flowering the seed capsules develop with smooth surfaces, squarish and with no wings.

F. acmopetala is one of the easier species, increasing reliably under garden cultivation. It is common in the vineyards and grain fields of Cyprus, Turkey, Lebanon and Syria. Its habitats range from sea level to approximately 1,200m (4,000ft) and it is usually found growing on stony limestone in scrub or light woodland. In gardens it will enjoy full sun or dappled shade with an open, well-drained soil and will soon make a beautiful clump, flowering in mid- to late spring.

F. a. wendelboi This is a recent introduction that is not as yet widely available. The stems grow only to 10cm (4 inches) and the leaves are broader, grey-green and fewer. The flower colour appears more stable, green and maroon topped by a darker purple band. It is a delightful dwarf flowering in late spring, an obvious candidate for the rock garden.

F. acmopetala is usually seen with a single flower as shown here, but it can have two or three to a stem.

F. a. alba An ivory-white form with brown margins has been sighted a few times but to date none have found their way into cultivation.

Fritillaria affinis
(6C) Pursh: tri: N. Am: syn. *F. eximia, F. floribunda, F. lanceolata, F. lunellii, F. mutica, F. ojaiensis.*
This is the third most widespread fritillary in North America. It increases quickly in the wild. The bulb is solid, round and pointed with numerous rice grains like baby bulbs around the base and side. The stem height is very variable, from a dwarf form at 20cm (8 inches) to giants at 80cm (32 inches), but the more usual height is 40–60cm (16–24 inches). The leaves are always held in whorls and although there are forms with a slate grey-green bloom covering the foliage, the leaves of the typical species are a glossy grass-green. They are broad and long, lanceolate, but become linear towards the top of the stem. The flowers are held in the leaf axils, up to 12 per stem, and each bloom is semi-pendant but with an open face. They are probably the most variable of the genus. In the wild *F. affinis* produces patches of plants of different forms that are all clearly closely related but cause problems when trying to define colourings; there are light and dark green forms with a large proportion of the open face painted and splashed with maroon, purple and black, but sometimes the colour ratios are reversed with the maroon and purple taking on the more prominent role while the flecks and lesser areas of lighter colour are a limy green-yellow. All the petals are fluted, in some the whole flower appearing rippled as if made of crêpe paper. The trifid style, divided in three, is so strongly recurved as to curl back on itself. The nectary is deep green. Many, if not most, forms have a high degree of sterility but when a capsule does form it is short and chubby, oval to cylindrical with dried wings on four sides.

This is a splendid plant for a sink, trough or tub. It needs a well-drained soil and a position where the flowers have dappled shade. Wild plants are widely distributed from south-west Canada down through California to Los Angeles, found in coastal scrub but also ranging up to yellow pine forest at 1,500m (5,000ft). If you are prepared to accept variable flower colours you will find this a magnificent addition to the late spring garden.

F. a. tristulis This plant is becoming very popular in gardens but is almost extinct in the wild. As it multiplies quickly in pots by producing large quantities of rice grains around the main bulb it is not difficult to bulk up a stock. This is a much shorter plant than is usual for the species, growing to 20cm (8 inches) with the upper leaves thin and grey-green; the lower ones are deeper matt-green and are broader. There are fewer flowers per stem than the type, only 1–3 bells, each coloured dark purple-black and beautifully finished with a grey bloom. The faces are virtually without detectable markings.

F. a. 'Limelight' A selected form that has been micro-propagated and recently offered. The stem rises to 40–60cm (16–24 inches). The leaves are dark green and the flowers an attractive lime green flecked with darker green.

F. a. 'Wayne Roderick', syn. Marin County form. A race found only in Marin County, California, where it grows with *F. liliacea*. The flowers have distinctive pointed petals and square shoulders with prominent angular nectaries. Colour can vary from brown chequered green, and with attractive green tips to the petals, to a form which is almost black but chequered brown or red. Not at present in commerce but becoming more widely spread among keen growers.

Fritillaria agrestis
(6B) Greene: tri: Calif.

This plant is related to *F. liliacea* and *F. biflora*. The bulbs are formed of a number of lily-like scales measuring only 2cm (¾ inch) and should be handled with care as these scales are loosely joined and although one broken off can be used to generate new stock the virility of the parent bulb will be impaired. The stem grows to 30–40cm (12–16 inches) and the yellowish-green leaves are paler than many, some with a serrated edge, an unusual feature in the genus. The foliage is clustered at the base, making a rosette of broad lanceolate leaves, with only a few much thinner leaves arranged alternately. The flowers possess an obnoxious odour from which comes the common name 'stinking bells'. There are usually 1–5 but occasionally as many as eight, depending on the strength of the bulb and the clone. The flowers are pendulous, open and recurved at the tips. There are two colour forms, a clear white with sulphur-yellow or green veining and a less sought-after one with muddy purple-brown flowers. The style is trifid, but the three parts are likely to be obscured by the prominent large yellow anthers. The nectaries are deep and outwardly protruding and the seed capsules are nearly square, held at an angle.

This makes a fine plant for a large, deep pot filled with rather heavy, even clay, soil. It revels in a hot, dry summer baking and resents soil disturbance. In the wild it is found in grassland at low altitudes and up to 150m (500ft) on heavy clay soils from Mendocino County to San Luis Obispo County, California. It is a worthwhile addition to any collection, blooming from mid-spring to early summer. In the open it will want a deep soil and a well-drained sunny spot.

Fritillaria alburyana
(1D) Rix 1966: e: Turkey: syn. *F. erzurumica*.

One of the few pink fritillaries in cultivation, this plant was named after S. Albury, who was on the expedition when it was discovered and who died collecting in Himalayas in 1970. The bulb has two scales joined by a central shoot, forming a rounded bulb with numerous bulblets. The stem is short, crocked or twisted and usually only 5–10cm (2–4 inches) with rarely more than two leaves. These are lanceolate, 4cm wide and 10cm long (1½ × 4 inches), grey-green and clasped around the stem. The flowers can look pathetic in cultivation if the winter has been mild. However, if this species receives a long period of cold winter temperatures and then a constantly warm, moist spring, the result is one bloom of magnolia pink chequered paler pink and white. The flower buds begin tubby and finally open to a wide saucer, revealing dark red anthers. There are variations to this typical colouring, some being a pale pink with little or no chequering. The petals can reverse backwards over the peduncle, quite unorthodox for a fritillary. The long style is featured prominently, either unbroken or with three lobes only sketchily suggested. The nectaries are creamy green, but not swollen; the capsules are smooth and without wings.

F. alburyana enjoys cool fresh water flowing over the bulb so it is important to keep the soil around the bulbs moist during the summer, quite the opposite treatment for most species. However, stagnant water is certainly not what is required. In the wild it is found growing in open screes, usually flowering by late snow patches in the north-central province of Erzurum, Turkey. It is a species highly thought of by growers, most highly prized for its late flowers that appear from late spring to midsummer.

F. a. alba Little is known of this uncollected plant. Its flowers are reported as being pure white or chequered with cream or pale green and the stem is reckoned to be taller than the type at 15cm (6 inches). The style is described as slender and more split, becoming trifid. Late spring to early summer flowering is followed by short, smooth seed pods.

Fritillaria alfredae
(1D) Post: e–lobed: Asia Minor.

This beautiful slender species from Lebanon is scarce in cultivation. A very small twin-scale bulb supports a wiry stem 15–30cm (6–12 inches) high. The long, broadly lanceolate leaves are a vivid green and arranged alternately up the stem but with a whorl of three leaves at the top surrounding and overhanging the flower. This is a solitary narrow tube 4–5cm (1½–2 inches) long, produced mid-spring. The light green outside colour is enhanced with a light hazy covering of

F. alfredae glaucoviridis, which comes from limy clay and stony fields in central southern Turkey and Syria.

glaucous blue, but this gives way to a darker green at the base near the peduncle. Towards the petal tips, which are gently reflexed, the colouring becomes lighter. Inside, the flowers are a pale green with the nectaries clearly smooth, not raised. The thick style usually ends lightly lobed rather than having a full-scale division into three. The seed capsules are squat with flaky dried wings.

F. a. platyptera (Samuelsson). A plant from Turkey and Syria and very similar to the type.

F. a. glaucoviridis (Turrill), syn. *F. a. haradjianii*. Also from Turkey and Syria and similar to the type, except that the flowers are more open to form campanula-like bells, pendulous and solitary. The outsides are a polished but rather dull green, becoming yellowish towards the tips, which recurve outwards. Inside the colouring is a light lime green and the nectary is deeply pitted. This plant is found in the wild growing in limy clay and in open stony fields of Adana, central southern Turkey.

Fritillaria ariana

(4) (Losina-Losinskaya) Rix: tri or absent: Asia.
F. ariana is for the experienced fritillary collector, being a rare and difficult plant like its close relative *F. gibbosa*. The stout stem is 25cm (10 inches) high with thin,

twisted, grey-green leaves arranged alternately, clasping the stem. Wide-open starry flowers stare outwards to display faces that are predominantly pink. It can usually produce 3–5 flowers per stem. Outside they are black with green edges but with the outer two-thirds mottled light and dark pink. Inside the dark pink becomes muddy pink towards the centre with deeply humped nectaries.

The species hails from Afghanistan and blooms in British gardens from late spring until early summer. It is best grown in a pot with a 50:50 mixture of peat with sharp sand and then given greenhouse space over winter and brought outside for a summer baking.

Fritillaria armena

(1D) Boissier: e: Asia Minor:
syn. *F. brevicaulis, F. tulipifolia*.

Sadly this plant is becoming rare in its native habitat in eastern Turkey, which is particularly unfortunate in view of the slow rate of increase of the small number in cultivation. The bulb is a small elongated one of two scales so closely fused as to appear a single solid unit. The stem is in the 4–7cm (1½–2¾ inches) dwarf range and is accompanied by 3–4 dusty grey-green leaves. The lower leaves are broad and erect, lanceolate, while the upper ones are also erect but linear. The pendant flowers are like grapes 2.5cm (1 inch) long, flaring at the mouth as they age. Two colour forms are recognized: the most frequently seen is a glossy damson colour overlaid with a grey sheen near the nectaries. The flowers inside are rich purple. The second form is a rusty orange with a touch of green on the outside, lighter orange to red on the inner surfaces. The nectaries are little more than small black token bumps. The style is broad and unbroken. The filaments are hairy and expanded and the seed capsules are long and smooth without wings.

In a trough or tub this species grows easily; the main requirement is protection from the summer rain. Given the right conditions it will flower regularly in early to mid-spring. In the wild *F. armena* is found growing around the snowline at 1,700m (5,500ft) in damp alpine meadows. It is a delightful small plant that takes up very little room in the garden.

F. a. caucasica A slightly more robust plant with very erect foliage clasping the taller stems at 5–20cm (6–8 inches), with 5–7 deep green, broad, long, lanceolate leaves almost entirely hiding the stem. The flowers are larger than the type at 3cm (1¼ inches) long, conical with slightly flared tips. The outsides are reddish-brown, lighter towards the edges; the insides are sulphur-yellow with slight green veining. There is a rare yellow-green form but this may not be in cultivation. The filaments differ from the type in being hairless.

While increase is very slow, the plant itself is reliable. It is found growing at an altitude of 2,700m (9,000ft) in the Mount Elbruz region of Caucasia. In the garden the flowering spike will begin to appear in mid-winter, especially if grown in a cold greenhouse, alpine house or protected bulb frame. It makes sense therefore to pay some attention towards preventing hard frosts damaging the precious flower buds. This is one of the first kinds to bloom, opening late winter to early spring.

F. assyriaca, which increases rapidly by bulbs and also produces plenty of viable seed.

F. a. zagrica (Stappf.) A dwarf form found in the Zagros mountains of Iran at 2,400m (8,000ft), apparently not at present in cultivation. The stem is only 6cm (2½ inches) tall with two leaves, a lower lanceolate one and an upper linear one held around the solitary flower. This is chocolate-coloured with a pale yellow-green patch at the tip of each petal. The three broad outer petals recurve and are shorter than the inner ones, which are narrower and straight.

Fritillaria assyriaca
(1D) Baker: e: Asia Minor.

F. assyriaca has been associated and confused with *F. uva-vulpis* for many years; in this book they are treated as separate plants. *F. assyriaca* has an elongated bulb of two scales to which are attached tiny stolon-like baby bulbs. The stem is thin and weak, 20–25cm (8–10 inches) tall and barely strong enough to hold aloft the weight of a solitary bloom. If 3–4 flowers are produced

the stem is likely to arch over, draping the flowers on the ground. The foliage gives the first clear indication that this plant is a distinct kind, with grey-green leaves that are held strongly and almost erect. The two lower leaves are broad and long, lanceolate, while the upper three or four are still lanceolate but somewhat thinner, arranged alternately up the stem. Narrow tube-shaped blooms are held in a semi-pendant pose, each a purple-brown with a metallic sheen, often slightly chequered green. They are 3–4cm (1 ¼–1 ½ inches) long with gently recurving petal tips which are edged light green. Inside the petals are highly glossy, a mix of green and brown with a broad straight style that dominates the centre by filling it. The nectary is slightly humped with no colour deviation, and the seed capsule is smooth and without wings.

This is a rapidly increasing plant from eastern Turkey and northern Iraq. After flowering in mid-spring it will set down many bulbs and produce abundant seed regularly each year. A large clump can soon be achieved in the open garden, especially if aided by a little spring frost protection. The ideal soil would be a leafmould-rich one in a moist spot where bulbs will flourish if undisturbed.

F. a. melanthera This is a smaller plant in all its parts and really requires a place in an alpine or cold greenhouse. The bulb is only the size of a pea and is made of two scales. The deep grey, thin stem is covered in a grey bloom and reaches only 10cm (4 inches) with deep grey, narrow leaves each twisting along its length.

The flowers are pendulous and deeply recurved at the mouth; inside they are striped purple and green and have black anthers and a broad, fat, entire style. The nectaries are humped on the outside and black inside. *F. a. melanthera* comes from the sandy, rocky hills near the coast of south-eastern Turkey.

Fritillaria atropurpurea
(6C) Nuttall: tri: N. America.

This is the most widespread of American species and it is not surprising that there is some variation. The bulb can be round to pear-shaped and is a solid structure with up to 50 rice grain bulblets. The stem is usually tall, some 40–60cm (16–24 inches), and finds support from the scrub among which it can grow; however, there are some dwarf forms as low as 25cm (10 inches). Grass-like

leaves are scattered irregularly along the stem, long and narrow and with rounded points. The lowest three have a light grey bloom overlaying their basic light green. The flowers are most often solitary or in pairs but it is not unusual for there to be 4–8 to a stem – though such profligacy is likely to be the death of the central bulb. The nodding blooms are reddish-brown with chequered splashes of green, greenish-white, yellowish-green or ivory, some with a delicate grey-blue sheen. As the flowers mature you will notice each pointed petal becoming wider and the long yellow anthers being more prominently displayed – often being longer than the petals. The clearly seen style is divided in three and generously recurved. The seed capsules are winged and have flat tops.

With such a wide distribution through 12 of the American states, it is surprising that this plant is not well represented in cultivation. In the wild it is found growing in light pine and fir woodland, in clearings and edges among stones and dwarf shrubs. It has also been found in sand dunes and certainly it always picks a dry, sandy or stony soil for its home. This is likely to be anywhere up to 3,000m (10,000ft) in places covered in snow for a long winter period. The seed is widely available and will germinate readily to grow into flowering specimens within four years. It blooms in mid-spring to early summer. It needs little moisture in summer and to be well-drained and cool through the winter.

F. a. pinetorum (Davidson) While it is botanically close to the type this is of much sparser distribution, found growing in the desert slopes of south Sierra Nevada and the thin pine forest up to 3,000m (10,000ft). The stem reaches 50cm (20 inches) with thin dark green and grey leaves whorling around the stem. The 3–8 flowers are slightly more open and face more outwards than the type. They are mauve-purple chequered lime. The bulb and style are similar to the type; the seed capsules are winged and carry four pointed horns on their tops. It is a late spring to early summer flower.

Fritillaria biflora
(6B) Lindley: tri: N. America:
syn. *F. ineziana, F. inflexa, F. succulenta.*

This is the chocolate bells, black fritillary or mission bells from the grasslands of the USA, particularly in Los

Angeles County, California. The bulbs are 2.5cm wide by 3cm deep (1 x 1¼ inches), composed of lily-like scales and completely devoid of rice grains. The stem is 25–40cm (10–16 inches) tall with a conspicuous basal cluster of lime-green polished lanceolate leaves each up to 4cm (1–1½ inches) wide. Above are a few scattered thinner ones with usually, but not always, one or two above the flowers. The norm is a pair of flowers although occasionally as many as six may be produced. Each is 3cm (1¼ inches) long, wide open and flaring at the mouth. The colour varies; most usual is a glossy amalgam of dark brown and black with deep red shading, but there are some with green shading or patchwork and with a green stripe. Inside a brown stripe marks each petal. The anthers are a similar length to the petals and the style is very clearly trifid with its three parts curling backwards. The elongated nectary is brightly coloured green inside and is raised on the outside; it makes its presence felt by exuding a pungent foxy aroma. The seed pods are smooth and unwinged.

This easy plant will be admired in the cold greenhouse or a protected trough, increasing slowly but flowering regularly. It seems to do best in heavy, compact loam. It responds well to a long summer drought extending to the beginning of winter; growth gets properly underway late winter to be followed by late spring blossom.

F. b. grayana (Reichbach fil & Baker), syn. *F. roderickii*. Fritillary growers know this plant well – it is a widely grown natural hybrid between *F. biflora* and *F. purdyi*, originally from heavy clay soils in Mendocino County, California, where it is now rare. The plant is much shorter than *F. biflora* with a stem of 10–20cm (4–8 inches) and the leaves are clustered at the base, being either grey-green or lime with no grey bloom. The flowers are late, usually early to midsummer, and have a notably obnoxious scent. Usually 3–4 reddish-brown flowers are displayed with central patches of creamy white, each like a hanging grape without any recurving tip. As it is of hybrid origin there is the expected variation. This would be an encouraging plant to start a seed-raising programme as it germinates freely and seedlings grow well.

F. b. 'Martha Roderick' A gorgeous selected form of *F. b. grayana*, this plant grows easily. Stout stems reach

F. bithynica is a delicate-looking and varied species from the Eastern Mediterranean region.

up to 20cm (8 inches) with lime-green leaves clustered at the base. The 3–5 flowers are brown but with the lower two-thirds taken up with a white patch. Inside the green-veined white petal surfaces are lacquered.

Fritillaria bithynica
(1D) Baker: e: E. Med.: syn. *F. citrina, F. dasyphylla, F. pineticola, F. schliemannii.*

This is a confusing species with numerous variations, some with recognized names but only slightly different from the type plant. Two closely clasped scales form a rounded bulb. The stem is 10–15cm (4–6 inches), with few leaves. The lowest two are short and wide, the middle and upper opposite pairs are thinner and longer; there is also a cluster of 3–5 leaves around the flowers, which are borne in early to mid-spring, usually in pairs

but sometimes single or in a group of three. They are narrow at their tops but broader at the mouth. Delicate colouring is achieved by overlaying the light green with a deep grey bloom on the outside while the inner surfaces are shiny and a lighter lime shade. The nectaries are green inside and only slightly humped outside. The style is short, thin and entire with a small hole in the centre; the seed capsule is long and thin with six flaky dried wings.

F. b. carica (Rix) While it is of similar stature to the type this form has differences which can be clearly seen when compared in bloom. The 10–15cm (4–6 inch) stem has broad lanceolate leaves arranged in pairs, opposite and with a grey bloom. There are no topknot leaves above the flowers. These are usually solitary but 2–3 may be produced. They are conical, wide open at the mouth and slightly recurving, a bright yellow, very rarely orange, and lightly veined green on the outside. The nectary is deeply pitted on the inside and deep green. The style is entire and partially covered with short hairs, and the seed capsules are without wings and smooth. This delicate small plant flowers very well in a cool greenhouse throughout the spring. It requires an open compost and a dry summer period. It hails from south-west Turkey, where it is found growing at 150–1,500m (500–5,000ft) in cedar forests.

F. b. carica serpenticola (Rix) This is a gorgeous dwarf plant for the alpine house or cold greenhouse, recently collected in south-west Turkey. It is only 2.5–7.5cm (1–3 inches) tall, with 2–3 grey-green leaves and small, open, conical flowers of deep golden-yellow. Though rather slow to increase it is a reliable mid-spring flower if grown in well-drained compost.

F. b. subalpina (Siehe) This form is a dwarf, only 5–7.5cm (2–3 inches) high, with lighter green flowers. It is not in cultivation at present.

F. b. viridiflora (Post) Unknown in cultivation, this form is said to be taller at 30cm (12 inches) and with deeper green flowers devoid of bloom.

F. bithynica carica serpenticola is one of the most highly regarded species for pot culture in either an alpine house or a cold greenhouse.

F. bithynica carica is from south-west Turkey, a slender plant with very pendant flowers which do not have any top-knot leaves. It is delicate but flowers well in a cool greenhouse throughout spring.

Fritillaria brandegeei

(6C) Eastwood: e: Calif: syn. *F. hutchinsonii*.

Beauty being in the eye of the beholder, this unusual kind may be admired by some; it is certainly interesting. The large, solid bulb is covered with rice grain bulblets. The stem is 60cm (24 inches) but often up to 90cm (36 inches) in the wild, where it grows through shrubs at the edge of woodland. The leaves are sparse, narrow and grey-green; they are held in whorls with one below each flower. The flowers are unlike those of any other

fritillary – up to eight of them are held as almost flat wide stars with anthers and styles jutting outwards. The petals are white with the black centre covering the nectary which is slightly raised on the outside. The anthers are black and the unbroken style white; altogether a most unusual American fritillary.

In the wild this plant is restricted to the southern Sierra Nevada mountains of California, where it is found growing in sharp, gritty soils at the edges of woods at altitudes up to 1,500m (5,000ft). In cultivation plants produce more flowers but increase slowly and flower later than in the wild, around midsummer. It is probably best in a cold greenhouse in well-drained soil.

Fritillaria bucharica
(4) Regel: e: Asia.

While this is a steady rather than rapid increaser it is one of the kinds more readily available in cultivation, being a reliable grower and bloomer. The bulb is large at 7.5cm (3 inches), rounded with two scales and rarely any bulblets. The stem is 20–30cm (8–12 inches) tall with large, broadly lanceolate, dull green leaves lower down and somewhat slimmer ones higher up. It is the complete opposite to the previous species in being very leafy, with the stem often completely obscured. While 8–10 flowers are the norm, there may be as many as 15 flat opened flowers assembled together towards the top of the stems. The small individual size, 2.5cm (1 inch), is made up for by the mass, all creamy white but usually with a definite hint of green. The nectary is clearly humped, a dark green outside and perhaps even darker inside. The thin thread-like style is entire but is sometimes completely absent. After the flowers fade their dried remains stay clinging on, the seed capsule growing within to form a smooth seed pod without wings and seedless.

This plant is from central Asia and northern Afghanistan, mainly found growing in stony clay soils up to 1,800m (6,000ft). In cultivation usually without seed or bulblets, the propagation of this plant is managed by splitting bulbs, treating the exposed surfaces with fungicide and replanting for the plants to re-form the opposite side within a season. This is one of the best

In the wild F. bucharica is found in central Asia and northern Afghanistan. It is one of the very best fritillaries for pot culture and will produce its creamy flowers reliably from mid- to late spring.

kinds for pot culture. It will bloom from mid- to late spring and thereafter needs a long dry summer.

Fritillaria camschatcensis
(6A) (Linnaeus) Ker-Gawler: tri: N. America, Asia.

Black sarana and Eskimo's potatoes are common names for this popular species, the only one to establish a transpacific status. It is a widespread plant, growing in eastern Asia, Japan, the west coast of Alaska, western Canada and northern parts of the USA. In the records of Captain Cook's voyage on the *Discovery* there is a note that dried roots of sarana were boiled and eaten like potatoes. This is not something to experiment with as fritillaries are often poisonous, especially in their raw state. The bulb is round, solid and 5cm (2 inches) across, the top half being covered with bumps, the lower half with many rice grain bulblets. The height is variable, but normally in the 20–40cm (8–16 inches) range. There are many whorls of shiny green leaves, always lanceolate, but broader at the base than up the stem.

This is usually the last fritillary to bloom, opening in mid- to late summer with up to four semi-pendant grape-like unpleasantly pungent flowers in dark purple or near-black shades. The interior colour is similar but lacquered and with contrasting creamy yellow anthers. This pigmentation is surprisingly constant for a plant of such wide distribution. The style is clearly trifid with the three divisions recurving strongly. The oval seed capsules are smooth and wingless. A very noticeable feature is the nectaries, which are deeply pitted inside and as black as night.

It is an easy plant outside, especially in slight shade and in humus-rich soils. It needs to be kept moist even after flowering, ideally with moving water below the bulbs; if they dry out and shrivel they will fail to reappear.

F. c. alpina There are several dwarf forms in cultivation, mostly Japanese forms under 15cm (6 inches); this is the name under which they are usually listed.

F. c. lutea This form is 30cm (12 inches) tall and similar in all respects to the type plant save in its colour, a lovely shining lime green-yellow. While scarce in cultivation it is well worth seeking.

F. c. multiflora A curiosity that is often listed as a double-flowering form as it has 8–15 petals loosely arranged around the pale yellow anthers. It flowers in midsummer and stands 30cm (12 inches) high.

Fritillaria chitralensis

(2) Wallich: tri: syn. *Petilium chitralensis*.

This is very similar to *F. imperialis* and is often classified under it. The bulb is large, 10cm (4 inches) wide, and consists of two scales with a hollow centre. It smells earthy but may not be as foxy as the genuine crown imperials. The stem is 50–70cm (20–30 inches) with light green leaves extremely abundant on the lower half of the stem, the upper half almost clear. They are all broad but there is a bunch of thinner ones as a topknot over the flowers. Up to four odourless blooms in bright golden-yellow open in mid-spring. The stem and leaves begin to appear in late winter, making it vulnerable to frost which can kill the flowering shoot. A cold greenhouse or similar protection is needed. This species is from around the Chitral Valley in north Pakistan, bordering Afghanistan and Kashmir.

Fritillaria chlorantha

(1D) Haussknecht & Bornmuller: e: Asia Minor.

In the wild this is beautiful but in cultivation it is difficult to recapture the same magic. It is a twin-scaled bulb with a stem 5–10cm (2–4 inches) tall. At ground level there are two very broad polished leaves, alternately arranged; above the flower there are 3–4 thinner, duller green leaves held erect around the flowers. These are usually solitary but occasionally in twos or threes. They are 2.5cm (1 inch) long, coloured grey-green on the outside and tipped purple at the mouth, inside shiny and a lighter yellow-green. The nectaries are smooth on the outside and green inside. The styles are unbroken.

This plant is closely linked to *F. bithynica* and can be found in the wild on the rocky slopes of the Zagros mountains of Iran, where it will often hybridize with *F. armena*. It is an easy plant and blooms in late spring, increasing very slowly in a loose well-drained loam best treated to a summer drought.

Fritillaria cirrhosa

(1B) D. Don: tri: Asia:
syn. *Guilelmi waldemarii*.

This is a wide-ranging plant with many variations. An oval twin-scaled bulb produces a stem 15–30cm (6–12

inches) tall. The leaves are always opposite but sometimes there are three not two. They are thin, grass-like and grass-green, each of the top ones having a short tendril tip. The flowers are pendulous and bell-shaped with pointed petals usually chequered yellowish or grey-green over a chestnut, mauve or purple background, but the ground and tessellation colourings can be reversed. All the stock available in cultivation has been raised from seed, thereby giving many coloured forms. The nectaries are raised on the outside and coloured a deep green inside. The style is trifid with the parts deeply recurving. The seed pods are smooth.

F. cirrhosa comes from the Himalayan range in Nepal and south-western China, growing at 3,000–4,500m (10,000–15,000ft). While easy to raise from seed, it is not so easy to keep growing from one season to the next; try it outside in a stone trough with well-drained loam, sharp grit and washed pebbles. The bulbs enjoy a cold winter, wet spring, dry summer and a wet autumn. It truly is one of the best fritillaries, being in bloom from late spring to early summer.

F. c. bonatii (S. C. Chen)
F. c. ecirrhosa (Franchet)
F. c. viridiflora (S. C. Chen)
F. c. roylei (Hooker)

Some experts consider these to be different forms but as they vary only by shades of colour and slight differences of height this may be overly pedantic. Only one must be treated as distinct and this is *F. c. roylei*, a tall fritillary 50cm (20 inches) high, the stem with scattered lanceolate leaves without any of the tendril tips of the type. The leaves tend to be bunched in fours or fives with a tuft of thin ones around the flowers. The stem arches somewhat with the weight of 3–7 blooms, dusky grey to brown and with a sweet honeysuckle scent. They persist in flower from late spring into early summer. This variety comes from Kashmir, where it is found growing at 2,400–3,500m (8,000–12,000ft).

Fritillaria conica

(1D) Boissier: tri: E. Med.

F. conica is one of the most delightful dwarf bulbs in cultivation. The bulb is small and rounded with two tight scales. The stem is 13–20cm (5–8 inches) high, strong, stout and very upright. The lowest leaves are at ground level, opposite, bright green on the underside

F. crassifolia is one of the easier species and is well worth growing in any of its forms. In its home of Asia Minor it is found in rocky mountains and limestone hills.

but grey-green on the upper surface and remarkably large for such a small plant at 4 x 10cm (1½ x 4 inches). They become thinner and shiny green as they ascend the stem, alternately arranged. The solitary flower is conical to grape-shaped, yellow with a hint of green on the outside but golden inside with the bright yellow anthers the same length as the deeply divided trifid style. The nectaries are smooth on the outside and green inside.

F. conica is becoming rare in its native habitat of southern Greece and the Peloponnese but may occasionally be found growing on limestone hills in scrub at 450m (1,500ft). Potted bulbs struggle to increase. It does better outside in full sun growing in well-drained light loamy soil, where it should flower regularly from mid- to late spring and increase steadily to form an eye–catching clump.

F. c. Rix 485 This form grown under Martin Rix's collection number is more or less identical with the type but the flowers are more open, being wider at the mouth than is usual.

Fritillaria crassifolia
(1C) Boissier & Reuter: tri: Asia Minor:
syn *F. ophioglosifolia*.

This is a very popular bulb, partly because it is widely available and increases easily but also because it just grows and grows – much less challenging than many fritillaries. The bulb is small with two scales to which one may expect to find small bulblets attached. The stem is usually 15–25cm (6–10 inches) tall but some forms can grow to 35cm (14 inches). The two lowest leaves are opposite, lanceolate and bright green; the 2–3 upper ones are alternate, thinner and glossy. The flowers are usually borne singly or in pairs and are large square-shouldered bells 4cm (1½ inches) across. Tessellation is a normal feature, being a faint green or brown chequering on the outside but a more intense clearly painted design of green and maroon-brown inside. The anthers are creamy white around the style, which is of similar length and very clearly trifid. The nectary inside is the starting point for a vivid green stripe that runs down the centre of each petal. The capsules are thin, elongated and without wings.

F. crassifolia is found in many places, in the rocky mountains of south-western Turkey, in the Lebanon and the limestone hills of Iran. It grows at 900–1,800m (3,000–6,000ft). It flourishes as a pot plant in an alpine house or cool greenhouse but is fine in the open rock garden, where it may be relied upon to bloom late spring to early summer.

F. c. kurdica (Boissier & Noe) Rix, syn. *F. foliosa*, *F. grossheimiana*, *F. karadaghensis*, *F. wanensis*. This is a smaller plant found growing around Lake Van in western Turkey. The stem reaches 10–12cm (6–8 inches) with up to eight larger and broader leaves reaching up and twisted to completely cover the stem. The flowers, tubby and bell-like, are slightly recurved at the mouth and are held in a cluster drooping over the leaves. You may expect 3–6 blooms per stem; usually the top

two-thirds are coloured maroon chequered yellow, the lowest one-third forming a bold yellow lip, though in some clones of *F. c. kurdica* this yellow lip may be absent. There is usually, but not invariably, a clear green stripe running down the length of the outer three petals. Because this is such an early flowering plant, opening late winter or early spring, it is best grown in a cold greenhouse or outside in a bulb frame with protection from winter frost that can damage developing flower buds and foliage.

F. c. poluninii (Rix) This plant is from northern Iran, but is almost extinct. The stem is 7.5cm (3 inches) only, with 5–7 thin green leaves clustered at ground level. The flowers are wide open and pure white with brown veining. It is probably not at present in cultivation.

F. c. hakkarensis (Rix) From the moist meadows of western Turkey and northern Iraq, this is a rare choice dwarf of only 5cm (2 inches) high with glossy leaves and evenly chequered flowers. The tessellation is in light green, brown and creamy green shades. The early to mid-spring blooms are wide open with the petals noticeably spaced; the stripes that are such a feature of the type are usually absent.

Fritillaria davisii
(1C) Turrill: tri: Greece.

F. davisii is one of the quickest increasers, often having 4–6 sizeable baby bulbs each year. These will take only 2–3 years to grow into good flowering specimens. The bulb has 2–3 small scales attached to a central shoot. The stem reaches only 8–16cm (3¼–6½ inches). Two notably broad leaves rest on the ground and the stem is then bare until the flowers, where there are 4–8 much thinner smaller leaves, closely gathered. The shiny green basal leaves measure 4–6 x 10cm (1¼–2¼ x 4 inches), huge for such a small plant. The pendulous or semi-pendulous flowers, of which there are 1–4, are dark chocolate outside and of a waxen texture; inside the yellowish-green shows lightly through to the outside petal tip. Some forms may have a light green chequered pattern or a pale green stripe on the outside. The nectaries are raised on each petal and are

F. crassifolia kurdica is a smaller form with flowers of varying colours. This yellow form is always admired.

F. crassifolia hakkarensis is a rare dwarf form from western Turkey and northern Iraq.

coloured dark green inside. The style is trifid but only in an understated manner.

This plant may be grown in a pot or outside in a trough or a scree-type spot in the rock garden, with 10cm (4 inches) of gritty mix over the bulb. It should then flower regularly in late spring and early summer. If you want quicker bulb increase the planting level can be shallower but this will be at the expense of flowering. *F. davisii* is found at low altitudes on hillsides up to 150m (500ft) in southern Greece.

Fritillaria delavayi
(1A) Franchet: tri: Tibet, Bhutan, W. Yunnan:
syn. *F. bonmaensis*.

High-priced seed of this beauty is for sale, but bulbs are more difficult to come by. It is a twin-scaled bulb producing a stem that is upright for 5cm (2 inches) when it arches and extends horizontally for a further 5cm (2 inches). The leaves are stone grey, thick and fleshy, the broad basal ones giving way to rather thinner ones towards the top of the erect part of the stem; the horizontal part is without leaves. The bell-like flowers face outwards and are coloured a stone grey suffusion over brown and peppered lightly with pale yellow. Inside they are a lighter brown with indented yellow-brown nectaries which are raised on the outside. The style is trifid in an understated manner. The seed pods develop with the wasted petals still in evidence, these capsules being short and smooth. When the seed is ripe the whole flower falls off, petals and all, and disperses the seeds through these retained petals. The seed should be sown on the surface of a well-drained gritty soil mix, perhaps 75 per cent grit to 25 per cent loam with a top dressing of sharp grit to a depth of 2.5cm (1 inch). For their first three years the seedling bulbs should never be wet nor completely dry. It could be another two years before the flowers appear in midsummer.

This rare dwarf fritillary is found on the stony scree slopes of Tibet and western Yunnan at around 3,000m (10,000ft). The colours blend in so well with the wild stony environment that many expeditions may have walked within metres of it without catching a glimpse of it.

Fritillaria drenovskyi
(1D) Degen & Stojanoff: tri: Balkans.

While available in cultivation this is almost extinct in the wild, where its home is the sparse pine and scrub areas of Bulgaria and Greece at altitudes of around 1,200m (4,000ft). It has many points of similarity to *F. armena*. Two or three small scales are joined to make a rounded bulb which produces a stem 20–25cm (8–10 inches) high. The alternate leaves are all very narrow and a deep grey-green. The small flowers, only 2cm (¾ inch) long, are deep purple and hang singly or possibly accompanied by 2–3 others. They are conical and slightly incurved towards the petal tips. Inside the purple is highly polished and forms an attractive backcloth for the yellow anthers.

The nectaries are elongated on the outside, and are black inside. The style is trifid, this breaking into three parts being the clearest distinction from *F. armena*. The seed capsule is smooth and with no wings.

This plant is slow to increase and requires special attention to its soil, which should be slightly moist during the summer and autumn. It likes a cool autumn followed by a cold (but not too wet) winter and a moist warm spring. Only in favourable years will it produce a number of baby bulbs, but it is very regular with its flowers, which appear in early to mid-spring without fail.

F. d. rixii (Zajarof). This form is vastly superior, and may be only loosely linked with *F. drenovskyi*. It has a 7.5cm (3 inch) stem and flowers 3cm (1¼ inches) long and wide, bright yellow both inside and out. It blooms from late spring into early summer. Its only habitat is Euboea, Greece, where it often hybridizes with *F. euboeica*.

Fritillaria eduardii
(2) Regel: e: Tadzikistan:
syn. *F. imperialis eduardii*, *Petilium eduardii*.

This plant has arisen as a hybrid between *F. imperialis* and *F. raddeana*. While found quite often in Tadzikistan, it appears not to be in cultivation. The genuine plant is described as having unscented bulbs, stems and foliage. The bulb is of two scales with little or no indentation in the centre. The stem is 60–75cm (24–30 inches) tall with alternate foliage spaced evenly along the stem, unlike *F. imperialis* with its clear stem. There are a few leaves over the flowers, which are pendulous, wide open pale orange bells with a slight recurve. The purple nectary may display a clear watery droplet of nectar. The style is entire and the seed capsule large, squarish and with a dried wing at each of the four corners. It blooms mid to late spring.

Fritillaria ehrhartii
(1C) Boissier & Orphanides: e: Greece.

This is another species of the tangled *F. bithynica* group, this one having clearly different-coloured flowers. The bulb is elongated and twin-scaled, and the stem can rise to 20cm (8 inches) but more usually measures 10–15cm (4–6 inches). The bottom two of the alternate leaves are broad but all the others are linear. The upper surfaces are glossy, the underneath a dull green. While occasionally there can be up to five flowers, the norm is

1–2 deep purple ones made more interesting by a lovely grey bloom. It is difficult to resist touching but if the petals are fingered the bloom comes off and the flower appearance is spoilt. The petal ends are marked with the tiniest dot of yellow and recurve slightly. Inside the glossy rich lime colour is veined deep green with the nectary hardly visible and completely unmarked. The anthers are yellow and the style is usually undivided, though three lobes may sometimes be lightly sketched. The seed capsule is smooth and unwinged.

This pretty little plant comes from the south-western isles of Greece, especially Euboea, where it is found at low altitudes of 150m (500ft) in heather and oak scrub on stony non-limestone soils. The flowers appear in early spring, making it wise to afford the plant some frost protection in pots or perhaps even better in a bulb frame with good drainage and an open-textured soil full of peat and grit. The bulbs tend to bury themselves deep to keep cool.

Fritillaria elwesii

(1D) Boissier: tri: Turkey: syn. *F. sieheana*.
The twin-scaled bulb of this plant is rounded and is usually soon accompanied by tiny ones around the base. The stem, which is thin and may need a little support, grows 25–40cm (10–16 inches) tall with alternate grey-green, thin leaves, long at the base and short near the flowers. One to three blooms are held rigidly in a semi-pendant pose, each being a narrow tube about 2cm (1 inch) long. The outer three petals recurve gently and are almost entirely green with only a thin purple edge. The inner three are purple-black and have no inclination to recurve, their outer surfaces being generously treated with a steel-grey bloom. Inside the flowers remain purple but a green line is drawn from the base down the centre of each petal and is clearly seen at the rim of the outer petals. The centre of the flower is filled with the yellow anthers and the broad, hairy style which may be lightly lobed but is clearly entire. The nectaries are black, outside slightly humped and giving the impression that the flowers are triangular. The seed pods are smooth, long and thin.

F. elwesii is widespread through south-western Turkey, where it can be found in pine woodlands up to 900m (3,000ft). When the flowers appear in mid- to late spring this species may be confused with *F. acmopetala* and *F. latakiensis*. In the wild they grow close together, sometimes overlapping in their distribution and here

F. euboeica has very showy colour. This flower is a mature one, very much more widely expanded than when young.

cross-pollination will occur. Hybrids may be detected in the wild with some care, but cross-pollinated seed brought into cultivation is likely to cause confusion. This plant likes open-textured soil to give good drainage and plenty of air but it should also be rich in humus. It will respond positively to an annual mulch of compost.

Fritillaria epirotica

(1C) Turrill & Rix: tri: Greece.
F. epirotica is rare and is not at present in cultivation, though it has been so in the past and there may be one or more odd plants tucked away in someone's collection, quite likely labelled *F. graeca*. The stem is a mere 7.5–10cm (3–4 inches) with a cluster of 4–5 leaves at ground level, none on the stem and a final bunch of 4–5 held over the flowers. These leaves are grey-green and are curiously twisted like a spring, a remarkably clear diagnostic feature. The flowers are relatively large at 3cm (1¼ inches) across; they are a dark bronze or brown, chequered lighter shades and with prominently

F. euboeica, a native of southern Greece, is more normally seen with a single flower to the stem. Its bright yellow blooms appear in late spring and although it is quite easy to obtain it does not yet have the popularity it deserves.

raised nectaries. Inside the flowers are lighter but the nectary is purple to black. The style is deeply cut.

F. epirotica is found on fast-draining rocky mountain slopes in north-western Greece at altitudes around 2,500 (8,000ft). The soil dries out soon after the early summer flowering, with the bulbs then resting until late autumn.

Fritillaria euboeica
(1D) Rix: tri: Greece.

This is often listed with *F. bithynica*, to which it is closely related. The bulb is very small, with two joined scales, altogether about the size of a pea. The stem is 7–10cm (3–4 inches) tall with two large leaves measuring 2 x 8 cm (¾ x 3¼ inches) at ground level. The other leaves, arranged alternately along the stem, are lanceolate, erect and often twisted once along the length. The foliage colour is a dark green overlaid by a light grey. The usually solitary flowers are grape-shaped but with petals slightly recurving as the blooms mature. Outside the green base over the nectaries gives way to a glowing yellow more or less all over. Inside the yellow is decorated with green veining and is deeper towards the nectaries. The style is definitely divided into three and the seed capsule is smooth and without wings.

F. euboeica belongs to Euboea in southern Greece, where it is found on limestone screes at 450m (1,500ft). Very little has been written about this gorgeous bright yellow dwarf and although the plant is available it is not yet widely appreciated. It blooms in late spring and does well in gritty loam that is allowed to dry out during the summer.

Fritillaria falcata
(6C) (Jepson) Beetle: tri: Calif.

This is perhaps the most startlingly colourful of all fritillaries. It has many points of affinity with *F. atropurpurea*, although it would be difficult to realize this at first glance. The bulb is fleshy with many tiny rice

grains attached around the base. It sheds these constantly when handled but experience seems to show it is an advantage if they can be left on the plant, all strength rallying to nourish the flowering stem. Removing these rice grains gives rapid increase but seems to be at the expense of the flowers. The stem usually grows to only 2.5–7.5cm (1–3 inches), but there are some forms which can double this. Most of the leaves are clustered at ground level, each being thick and fleshy with a stone-grey bloom covering the surface. The lower leaves are opposite, the upper ones alternate with sometimes a single one over the flowers. These are star-shaped, wide-open and facing outwards from the stems at 60–90°, showing their beautifully coloured faces. The predominant pigment is red or chestnut with a creamy green edge, this red backcloth being circled and splashed with cream, yellow and green. Unusual brown anthers are held horizontally over the petals. The nectaries are dark green inside and slightly raised outside. The style is trifid to the degree of splitting down its complete length. The seed capsules develop with small curled horns, these being the remnants of the style, something that is more usually found with tulips.

Unhappily there is a real danger of most populations being grazed to extinction, but there are a few isolated patches growing in coastal situations on the steep mountain screes of southern California at a height of 900m (3,000ft). While there seems to be plenty of stock in cultivation it looks as if at present nurserymen are holding their stock to grow bulbs to flowering size. If you can obtain it you will find this a rewarding plant, flowering in late spring to early summer. It must have a perfectly drained gritty soil, preferably in a deep pot so that it can be thoroughly baked in the summer. In autumn remove the top 2.5cm (1 inch) of soil only and replace it with fresh nutrient-enriched compost. Keep in an alpine house, cool greenhouse or frame over the winter.

Fritillaria fleischeriana
(1D) Steudel & Hochstetter: e: Turkey.
This plant is found in eastern Turkey and Iran at 900m (3,000ft) on west-facing slopes. Little is known about

F. falcata, one of the most startlingly coloured of the American species, is now unfortunately under threat in its wild habitats in California.

this species, and though it was once grown in Denmark by Ole Sonderhousen it may well not be in cultivation now. It has small twin-scaled bulbs and a stem no higher than 7.5cm (3 inches) tall. The few narrow leaves are covered in a grey bloom, the lowest two opposite, the remainder alternate. Late spring flowers are usually solitary but pairs are possible. They are narrow and pendulous, their dark purple being marked with light green outside. Inside they are lighter, an amalgam of yellow and brown but with green nectaries. The style is entire. Further research is awaited.

Fritillaria forbesii
(1D) Baker: e: Turkey.

This delightful little plant is a favourite with many bulb growers. Although *F. forbesii* is often classed with *F. bithynica* it is probably even closer to the species *F. rhodia*, with confusion in labelling being not uncommon. The bulb is small and rounded, with two scales supporting a very thin stem that reaches 15–20cm (6–8 inches), with thin twisted grass-like leaves. While in cultivation these are usually grass-green, in their natural habitat plants growing in full sun have usually quite grey leaves with those in shady spots a light green. The 1–3 small pendant flowers are 2cm (¾ inch) long, a more or less uniform bright yellow although the nectaries may have a slight green sheen outside and be pale yellow or green inside. The three inner petals are held formally downwards but the outer three are very generously recurved at the mouth. The style is almost rudimentary, very short, entire and quite difficult to see. The seed capsules are smooth and without wings.

F. forbesii is widely available. It is easy to grow in a gritty loam which is allowed to dry out during the summer, but the bulbs increase only slowly and this can mean a high price for the initial purchase. Plants bloom successfully from early to mid-spring if grown in deep pots housed in a cold greenhouse. In the wild it struggles in the face of the onslaughts of human development, being especially vulnerable at the relatively low altitudes it inhabits in southern and western Turkey from sea level to 300m (1,000ft), usually in stony rocky scrubland. There are no named forms but there is a deeper orange form which appears from time to time, in all other particulars being identical to the type.

Fritillaria gibbosa
(4) Boiss.: tri: Asia Minor.

While this attractive species from Iran and Afghanistan was offered by several nurserymen in the late 1980s it proved to be depressingly difficult and most bulbs soon failed. A few persist in specialist collections and it may be possible to obtain some, especially if the grower thinks there is a chance of the purchaser succeeding with the plant. The stem grows to 7.5–20cm (3–8 inches). The lowest leaves, at soil level, are an earth brown or grey colour, of thick fleshy texture, lanceolate and measuring about 4 x 8cm (1½ x 3¼ inches). The upper leaves, held close to the flowers, are the same colour but thin and rippled, twisted or curled. Three to six blooms face outwards with their petals slightly recurving. Pigmentation is extremely varied, most usual being pink shades from pale to rose pink, although occasional individuals are brick red or apricot. The nectaries are deep red on the outside and are a characteristic feature of this complex of species, being grand enough to measure 0.5–1cm (¼–½ inch) long in *F. gibbosa*. They are highlighted by a deep purple circular band around them on the inner surfaces of the petals. The anthers fall in with the colour scheme by being brown or red. The style is very short and trifid but not dramatically so. Often the style is missing and obviously these flowers will have no seed; where fertile seeds are set these will be contained in short, fat round capsules with wings.

Native to steep slopes at 900–1,800m (3,000–6,000ft) in Iran and Afghanistan, this plant needs certain conditions to survive and then flower in late spring to early summer. It seems to do best in a cold greenhouse, growing in deep pots of grit and sieved loam. The summer should be dry, possibly spent in a covered frame with only the plunge material receiving the very minimum of water. In the autumn it can be placed outside to receive a little moisture followed by a cold dryish winter in a covered frame. In the early spring it can be brought inside the greenhouse and watered, carefully monitoring the amounts so that it is never dry nor sodden.

Fritillaria glauca
(6C) Greene: tri: N. America.

This golden-flowered fritillary is a distinct character well differentiated from the other American species, though it may be related to *F. purdyi*. Seed is fairly widely available and soon it will be entering the lists of bulb-growing nurserymen. The bulb approaches the lily form with similar scales and at the base a few bulblets. The stem is 7.5–13cm (3–5 inches) tall with lanceolate leaves at ground level, these being a basic pale green to grey but distinguished by a blue-grey bloom that, protected by glass, will overlay all, though it is easily marked by rain, overhead watering or a fingertip. The large late spring or early summer flowers are solitary and wide but not exaggeratedly so. On the outside the petals are waxen, golden-yellow and with highly raised nectaries shaded buff or brownish-yellow. Inside the gold is heavily flecked with brown and there are chocolate patches around the nectaries. While this is the standard colour scheme, there are rare individuals coming close to an orange-brown or chestnut-red. There may be a small gathering of short hairs at the base of each nectary. The deep yellow anthers are as long as the petals, and the style is split into three along its whole length. The seed capsules are held at a 45° angle and have conspicuous broad dried wings.

The wild plant is found plentifully from Oregon into north-west California, growing in alpine rocky screes at 600–2,100m (200–7,000ft). Its distribution overlaps that of F. purdyi, which blooms later and has unwinged seed capsules. F. glauca is best grown in an alpine house or cold greenhouse in open gritty loam that drains freely. It can be allowed to dry out during the summer, but when raised from seed it is important to keep the soil moist to the touch year-round for the first two years.

Fritillaria graeca

(1C) Boissier Spruner: tri: Balkans: syn. F. guicciardii, F. ochridiana, F. unicolor, F. urmensis, F. zahnii.
This is a complex and interesting group of colourful easy plants. The typical form can be variable in size and flower colour, so giving rise to a number of misnamed varieties. It has a bulb with two closely clasped scales and a stem which averages some 20cm (8 inches) in height. Often seed collected in the wild will give a wide scatter of different heights among the seedlings, the smallest being about 10cm (4 inches) and the tallest 35cm (14 inches). Broad leaves at the base give way to alternate grassy narrow ones above, all covered with a pale grey bloom. Taxonomic problems arrive with the flowers. Solitary or paired blooms of the typical form can merge with F. davisii, F. pontica and F. messanensis, a motley group. The colour schemes are always in green

and red, but it is not easy to distinguish where one species ends and another begins. Typical F. graeca petals each have a central green stripe with a light, brick or brownish-red to the sides with some forms chequered green and others not. The petals can incurve slightly but less than in F. pontica and F. messanensis where they also curl outwards gently; in F. davisii the petals are straight. While the green stripe is retained inside, the rest of the surface is more definitely chequered green. The nectary is overlaid with a black patch. The anthers are yellow and the style is deeply divided; the seed pods are smooth and without wings. Unfortunately the smell of the flowers is like that of none-too-fresh raw meat. This attracts wasps, which help the pollination process but can be a nuisance in a conservatory or elsewhere under cover. This is an encouragement to get bulbs growing outside as soon as possible, and this is one of the easiest fritillaries for borders, rock gardens or troughs.

F. graeca is to be found in various places through central and northern Greeece into southern Bulgaria, especially on rocky slopes and in dappled shade at altitudes up to 2,700m (9,000ft). Individuals are in bloom for about three weeks, so with a mixture of clones there is the possibility of blossom from early spring until midsummer. The species is very much at home in British gardens, increasing and blooming every year when grown in suitable conditions. It should be planted 15cm (6 inches) deep in light shade from an almost overhanging shrub, a fence or a low wall. It likes a cold winter soil that becomes warm and moist in spring, this moisture remaining present through the summer and autumn. This is a readily available kind and should be high on the list of those making a starter collection; it is going to be more and more widely grown.

F. g. thessala (Boissier) Rix, syn. F. ionica, F. thessalica, F. pontica ionica. This is widespread and easily found in northern Greece, southern Bulgaria and in Albania. With similar but broader lanceolate grey-green leaves arranged alternately along stems, this form grows 20–30cm (8–12 inches) tall. The distinctive whorl of three grey leaves held over the flowers may suggest it is F. pontica, especially since the flowers at one end of the colour range closely resemble this species with no red borders, being all green except for a light lip of red or brown. At the other end of the range flowers are close to the type species with a broader green stripe down each

petal and a paler red border heavily chequered green. The nectaries inside have a large, more prominent black patch at the petal bases, while the styles remain trifid. The seed pods are smooth. This grows well in the garden but may increase better with a period of summer drought.

Fritillaria gussichiae
(1C) Degen & Dorfler: tri: Greece.

While for many years classed with F. graeca, this rare and difficult plant has more differences from than similarities with this species and is probably closer to F. pontica. The twin-scaled bulb supports tall thin stems 25–38cm (10–15 inches) high. Alternate leaves clasp the stem; they are lanceolate and are covered with a grey bloom. There is a little cluster of smaller ones with the mid-spring flowers, of which there are 4–6, incurving gently at their mouths and sulphur-yellow to pale green with grey overtones. The nectaries are shaded red on the outside. Inside, in the manner of many fritillaries, the colour is darker; the nectaries are black and this sprays out over the green and brown petal surfaces. The anthers are creamy yellow and the style distinctly cut into three. The seed capsules differ from those of F. graeca by having small thin wings in each corner in the manner of F. pontica.

This is a rare wild plant found occasionally in humus-rich deciduous woods in northern Greece at altitudes up to 1,200m (4,000ft). Although bulbs are sometimes offered under this name they usually turn out to be a F. graeca or F. pontica form; it is probable that the genuine plant is not in cultivation at present.

Fritillaria hermonis
(1C) Fenzl: tri: Lebanon.

This is the only fritillary where a variety is widely cultivated but the species is not listed in catalogues. F. hermonis has a very short stem, only 5–13cm (2–5 inches), with lanceolate grey-green leaves and flowers like slender bells chequered red and brown over dark purple. Inside they are deeper red to purple with short black nectaries only slightly raised. Blooming in late spring, it will need the same conditions as the variety F. hermonis

F. graeca thessala, a relatively widespread and variable form of a Balkans species that is one of the more amenable ones in British gardens. It is distinctive for the whorl of three grey leaves held over the flowers.

F. hermonis amana, an easy plant whether grown in a container or in the open garden.

amana. The only plants in cultivation would seem to be in botanical or specialist private collections. It comes from the Hermon mountains of Lebanon where it is found on screes and among rocks up to an altitude of 1,500m (5,000ft).

F. h. amana (Rix) This is an easy plant to grow in a pot, trough, rock garden or open border. It increases into a large clump with very little need for special encouragement. There is concern about the wild populations of bulbs being widely plundered in the Middle East and it may be that this is one that has been so exploited. Try to ensure when purchasing that you are not buying collected bulbs – there should be no need as this is a form

that increases well under cultivation. It grows wild in southern and eastern Turkey through Syria and into the Lebanon mountains. There are lovely colour forms, all seeming to be linked closely to those grown under the name F. crassifolia. The round twin-scaled bulb has a large number of bulblets around the base. The stem reaches 13–18cm (5–7 inches) high, with shiny grass-green leaves each 10 x 2.5cm (4 x 1 inches) and arranged alternately; the long, pendant, bell-like flowers have prominent raised nectaries and are a pale reddish-brown outside but with a central green stripe running the whole length of each petal, the red also being splashed or spotted with green. Inside the petals are a uniform lustrous lime-green with the nectaries a darker green. The thick style is trifid, and the seed pod is smooth. In late spring this plant can act as a focal point in the garden; after a few seasons substantial clumps will produce plentiful flowers. While enjoying a basic gritty soil, this plant relishes an annual topdressing of well-rotted compost.

F. h. amana Lebanese form This is a frequently offered selection with green flowers, the outer three petals being uniform green but the inner three having a band of light chestnut-red. In other respects it is similar to F. h. amana.

F. h. amana E. K. Balls 1034 This is recognized as the best form of F. h. amana, collected decades ago by E. K. Balls under the number 1034. While perfectly hardy outside it is so stunning that the temptation is to grow it in pots for easier viewing. The stem is shorter, only 10cm (4 inches), but carries large long bells 4cm wide by 5–6cm long (1½ x 2½ inches), the outer three petals being a dark green but with the under surface painted a dark red so intense that it shows lightly through to the outside. The inner three petals each have a central thin green stripe dividing the two blood-red sides, these recurving outwards far more than in the typical form. The undersurfaces of the inner petals are a darker green and red. In some individuals this red may not be present. The nectaries are always dark red on the inside and prominently humped on the outside.

F. hermonis amana lutea. F. h. amana is variable in colour, some being reddish-brown with green stripes, some an all-over limy shade and some, like this one, dominantly yellow.

F. h. amana lutea, syn. *F. h. amana* yellow form, *F. h. amana* 'Sunglow', *F. h. amana* the pale form. This is lime-green to lemon and is again smaller than the typical form at 13–15cm (5–6 inches) with dark green lanceolate leaves and pendulous flowers with petals that do not overlap and recurve. The lemony yellow colour has light green tessellation both inside and out. The humped nectaries are dark red to brown on the inside, this showing through to the exterior. This is a slightly more tender plant not so widely available and is probably best in a cool greenhouse.

Fritillaria imperialis

(2) Linnaeus: tri–lobed: Asia, Asia Minor.
This plant has been cultivated for almost 400 years after being introduced into Europe from Turkey via Vienna in the sixteenth century. It quickly became one of the essential hardy herbaceous plants and within 100 years of introduction there were 30 different forms available to gardeners; whites, purples, spotted ones, doubles, forms with silver- and golden-variegated leaves. Most have been long since lost, but there are still 10–12 forms to be found in various lists and up to 20 in the national collections and in private gardens.

The species is distributed over a 3,500km (2,000 mile) stretch of land from southern Turkey through northern Iran to Afghanistan and Pakistan. The typical plant has a really large bulb, measuring 13cm wide and 7.5–8cm long (5 x 3½ inches). They are rounded, with two or three very thick starchy scales and a prominent hole in the centre, marking where last year's flower stem was. The foxy smell that is a characteristic of most is not always present, though sometimes this scent can be evident even when growing. The very stout stem grows rapidly to 90–120cm (36–48 inches) in the strongest forms and is accompanied by a rather lush group of very broad leaves held fairly erect and obscuring the bottom third or half of the stems. The upper halves are clear of leaves up to the showy bunch of flowers, but above this is the prominent crown or top-knot tuft of shiny narrower leaves. Up to six large bell-shaped flowers are hung as a circle, orange or yellow in the wild and sometimes with somewhat darker veining.

F. imperialis 'Aureomarginata', a crown imperial grown as much for its variegated foliage as for its flowers. It is susceptible to frost in cold districts.

Inside the colour is at least as strong but with a black or very dark green patch around the white nectaries. Flowering period is mid- to late spring. If the flowering stem is tapped by hand a thimbleful of nectar can be collected. The style is as long as the petals and is three-lobed rather than divided. The squat, fat seed pods have four wings.

***F. i.* 'Aureomarginata'** Maybe a kind for the collector, as it can be expensive and tends to become frosted in cold districts. The orange flowers are veined red, but the distinguishing feature is the lemon edges to the top leaves. The height is 90cm (36 inches).

***F. i.* 'Aureovariegata'** An old kind that is difficult to find. The flowers are a deep orange-chestnut with a top-knot of green leaves edged silver-white. The height is 90cm (36 inches).

***F. i.* 'Aurora'** This blooms earlier and so is subject to frost damage in cold districts. The 60cm (24 inch) stem carries orange flowers veined red and with deep red nectaries. A clump looks clearly shorter and neater than many other forms. Ideal for a small garden.

***F. i.* 'Indora'** This is a rarity from Turkestan with a short stem of 60cm (24 inches) and bright yellow flowers. The bulbs appear to be free of the foxy smell. There is also a selected form with purple flowers, *F. i.* 'Indora Purpurea'.

***F. i.* *lutea*,** syn. *F. i. flava.* A bright yellow form with stems 90cm (36 inches) tall, the flowers having a faint green veining inside and deep green patches around the nectaries.

***F. i.* 'Maxima Lutea'** Very impressive and similar to *F. i. lutea* but with stems perhaps reaching 120cm (48 inches).

***F. i.* 'Maxima Rubra'** Similar to *F. i.* 'Rubra' but with taller stems, 120cm (48 inches) high.

***F. i.* 'Prolifera'**, syn. *F. i.* 'Crown-on-Crown' ('Kroon-op-Kroon'). A good form with 2–3 superimposed whorls of pale orange flowers on a stout stem 60cm (24 inches) high. There is often a light purple veining

on the exterior and the nectaries are deep green and white.

***F. i.* 'Rubra'** This plant quickly establishes a large clump with 90cm (36 inch) stems carrying dark orange-red flowers with deep maroon veining. Inside the nectaries are a deep red with a central white eye.

***F. i.* 'Sulpherino'** Recently rescued from oblivion by the Hortus Bulborumat, a garden at Limmen in the Netherlands devoted to the conservation of old bulb cultivars, especially tulips. The outsides are orange with purple veining, while the petal tips have a yellow margin and the nectaries are flushed purple. Unusually for a fritillary, the insides are a shade lighter but with nectaries purple and white. The height is 90cm (36 inches).

***F. i.* 'The Premier'** A plant with a stem around 60cm (24 inches) and early flowers that are clear red or dark orange with little or no veining.

Fritillaria involucrata
(1C) Allioni: tri–lobed: France, Italy.

This European species cannot be regarded as one of the most spectacular of the genus; nevertheless it is not without quiet charm and is a pleasing curiosity. It is one of the most popular of outdoor fritillaries, probably becáuse it increases and blooms so freely. The small rounded bulb has two scales that are drawn up to an elongated central point. The stem reaches 25–35cm (10–14 inches) high, with narrow, grass-like foliage that is covered in grey bloom. The lower leaves can form a mini-whorl of three or just two opposite ones. Above they are alternate up to the flowers, on top of which there is a whorl of three. The usual 2–3 flowers, borne in late spring, may occasionally reach a total of five bells, each gently opened at the mouth. The exterior surfaces are a pale apple-green modified with a little darker chequering towards the nectaries. Inside there is an intricate fishnet of black or reddish-brown lines embellishing the background green, the pattern being finished with black nectaries. The yellow anthers are short and are tucked behind the style which is lobed or lightly divided. The seed pods are slender, with rounded tops, containing very small seeds.

F. involucrata is close to *F. meleagris* and *F. messanensis* and will hybridize indiscriminately. This species is becoming scarce in the wild, now only being found in the remoter parts of the French and Italian Alps, where it grows on grassy limestone slopes at altitudes up to 1,200m (4,000ft). However, it grows well in gardens, especially given some summer shade. Like most European kinds it can benefit from the presence of a small deciduous shrub such as a lavender or the dwarf birch *Betula nana*. When planting it is worth giving it a handful of grit below and above. In autumn and winter it likes a mulch of compost.

Fritillaria japonica
(1C) Miquel: tri: Japan.

Although rare in cultivation *F. japonica* is not quite impossible to find. During the 1980s it was offered by a few nurserymen but it proved difficult, posing a challenge even to the experienced *Fritillaria* enthusiast. The bulb is virtually only a single scale tapering from a broad base to a pointed top and measuring about 4cm (1½ inches). The stem is 5cm (2 inches) high, accompanied by 3–4 narrow leaves, grassy-green and grassy-looking. The pendant solitary flowers are square-cut bells with sharply pointed petals, each of these being the purest white except for some brown chequering towards the outer nectary surfaces; inside is similar with the nectaries coloured a pale creamy brown. The style is trifid.

This Japanese species is found only sparingly in light shady woods where it grows in peaty leafmould. The flowers appear in late spring. It is very susceptible to frost damage and needs the rootrun to be moist and cool at all times, never soaking wet and never dry. A trowelful of washed grit below and above the bulb may help to keep it cool and not too wet in an open-structured soil made acid with peat and leafmould.

F. j. koidzumiana (Ohwi) Rix. Much the same as the type but perhaps slightly larger and with the tessellation much more definitely marked. It is more widely available but is still difficult, temperamental and expensive.

Fritillaria karelinii
(4) (Fischer) Baker: e: Asia.

This plant is close to *F. gibbosa* and in the wild there are places where the two produce hybrids. It grows in western China and central Afghanistan in semi-desert areas, and as yet there seem to be none in cultivation. The stem measures 15cm (6 inches) with grey-green leaves, sparse and alternate. The flowers are solitary, wide-open stars of rose pink with some deeper spots and veining. The nectary is prominently raised outside and deeply pitted inside. Apparently the flowers are more often without styles than with; when present these are straight and entire and may or may not be followed by short flat-topped seedpods that are smooth and wingless. The flowering period is mid-spring.

Fritillaria kotschyana
(1C) Herbert: tri: Iran.

This exciting large-flowered fritillary can be a star in the alpine house or cool greenhouse. It is closely linked with the *F. crassifolia* group. The twin-scaled bulb produces stems up to 15cm (6 inches) high, with only a few lanceolate alternate leaves which are all a glossy green. The lantern-shaped flowers measure 6cm (2½ inches), with petals pointing down and not overlapping. The exteriors are blood-red but with brown and green tessellation. The yellow anthers and divided style can be seen at the mouth of each flower.

F. kotschyana comes from the Elburz Mountains of northern Iran up to levels of 1,800m (6,000ft). It is not a difficult plant in free-draining gritty soils with the bulbs placed 10cm (4 inches) down in a deep pot. It helps the plant if it is shielded from frost in early spring as it comes into blossom. When the flowers and leaves have faded away keep the soil virtually dry until the early autumn.

Fritillaria latakiensis
(1D) Rix: tri: Turkey, Asia Minor.

While it has only been in cultivation for a decade this species has quickly become recognized as an easy garden plant, increasing steadily to make it popular with both gardeners and nurserymen. The twin-scale bulb is small and rounded with a few bulblets around the base; the stem reaches 25–40cm (10–16 inches) and displays narrow alternate leaves covered in a grey bloom dominating the underlying green. The 1–2 flowers are narrow with rounded shoulders tapering down to slightly flared mouths. Outside they may be purple or grey-purple with a central grey green stripe. With so tube-like a flower it is difficult to see inside, but here the petals are purple with a light green sheen. The style is divided, the nectaries are smooth and rounded on the outside, and the globe-shaped seed pods have no wings.

F. latakiensis is an up-and-coming easy species in gardens, given moisture and free drainage. It makes a graceful picture in rather sombre colours.

This plant flowers in the late spring or early summer and enjoys a spot where it will not dry out during the summer; it likes moisture, coolness and free drainage. Sometimes *F. latakiensis* is confused with two other species, *F. elwesii* and *F. acmopetala* (see under *F. elwesii*). *F. latakiensis* is found in Latakia in north-western

Syria but also in a narrow band westwards along the southern Turkish mountains to the Taurus range.

Fritillaria latifolia

(1A) Willdenow: tri: Turkey, Caucasus.
This is a very variable plant with disproportionately large blooms. It is possibly linked with other species, but itself has a large number of forms. While the species has been in cultivation over 300 years it cannot be described as popular or widespread, probably because it

lightest suggestion of it. The nectaries are deep purple and the style is deeply divided. The wingless seedpods are cylindrical.

Increase is very slow but it will bloom regularly in mid- to late spring, growing well enough in a trough or in a cold greenhouse in a deep pot of gritty loam. Try this one before venturing on to some of the rare varieties and forms. In the wild the species has a wide distribution in the grassy slopes of the Caucasus mountains and southern states of the former Soviet Union as well as in eastern Turkey.

F. l. aurea (Schott), syn. *F. aurea*. Often listed as a separate species, this is clearly close to the typical *F. latifolia*. The stems vary between 2–13cm (^{3}/$_4$–5 inches), with

F. latifolia collina, a golden form of a species which has been in cultivation for over 300 years.

is slow-growing and temperamental. From an oval bulb of two scales the stem grows 15cm (6 inches) high. The leaves are clustered up around the flower and are bright glossy green or a dull grey-green, the two bottom ones being oval, the rest narrow and hiding the top half of the stem. The flower is one of the largest of the genus, a square-topped single bloom with prominent raised nectaries tapering down towards rounded petals incurved at the mouth. The rich colouring is red or chocolate outside and red inside, with no patterning or only the occasionally the flowers lolling on the ground. These are box-shaped, with raised nectaries reinforcing the effect. Outside they are a uniform rich gold, inside there is some light brown peppering. This plant is not easy to grow, the main problem being to keep the soil moisture at the required level, which means just sufficient to start growth in the spring and dryish conditions for the rest of the year. Overwatering can kill. For this a pot is required, preferably a large one as the bulbs do not like rapidly fluctuating temperatures. Shading can help. It comes from central Turkey where it grows on limestone slopes.

F. l. collina (Adams). Taller at 20–25cm (8–10 inches), this is a golden-yellow Caucasian form with the outside spotted brown, the insides having deeper coloured tessellation in chestnut-red. If it were not for the longer stems this could look very similar to *F. l. aurea*, though *F. l. collina* also has more rounded shoulders and more sharply pointed petals.

F. l. 'Erasmus' This is a newly collected form about which little is known except that it has olive-green flowers which are chequered brown inside.

F. l. lagodechiana (Charkhorich). This plant is similar to the type, with a whorl of three leaves around the lemon or green flowers. It comes from northern Turkey and southern Georgia.

F. l. macedonica (Bornmuller). This plant collected in the eastern Alps has a dark brown to purple flower strongly chequered lilac. It is known through a specimen in the Berlin herbarium. It probably has close links to *F. tubiformis*.

Fritillaria liliacea
(6B) Lindley: tri: Calif.
This is a beautiful plant rather reminiscent of *Leucojum autumnale*, the autumn snowflake. The bulb is solid and elongated with a few rice grain bulblets at the base. The stout stem is 15–30cm (6–12 inches) tall, and clear of leaves between the basal rosette and the flowers. These bottom leaves are fleshy, narrow and polished, while the ones around the flowers are narrow and short. A sweet scent emanates from the wide-open creamy-white flowers with their narrow petals rounded

at the tips; 3–5 is a normal complement. They are borne in late spring and early summer. The nectaries are green inside and marked outside with green patches; a few small hairs are found around the base. The style is heavily divided and the seedpods are smooth and rounded.

This species grows in heavy clay grasslands in Marin County at low altitudes – perhaps only up to 30m (100ft). It is not one of the most difficult of the American species but it prefers a really stiff, limed clay in a deep pot that is kept free of frost in the winter but cool and dry in the summer, probably best outside in the shade. Availability varies – some years ago it was relatively easy to buy, but now its frost-tender reputation has lost it some popularity among nurserymen.

Fritillaria lusitanica
(1C) Wikstrom: tri: Spain, Portugal:
syn. *F. boissieri, F. hispanica, F. maria, F. stenophylla*.
This plant has so many similarities to *F. pyrenaica* that it could stand as a variety of this species. The bulb is a small one with two scales. The stem reaches 20–30cm (8–12 inches) with alternate linear leaves lightly touched with grey bloom well spaced along its length. The flowers could be mistaken for those of *F. messanensis*, with 1–4 hanging blooms like bells with flanged mouths. Outside the petals are mottled red and brown with a light green stripe bisecting each one and a touch of yellow on the lips; inside the colour is predominantly a chequered pattern of yellow and brown, with a heavier band of yellow around the lips. The nectaries are smooth outside and black inside. The style is divided with the yellow anthers tucked behind, and the seedpods are smooth and wingless.

A native from north-western Spain and northern Portugal in dry pine forest up to 2,100m (7,000ft), this plant is in cultivation but can be difficult to come by as it hybridizes freely with *F. pyrenaica*. The type and the hybrids are all good garden plants, growing and increasing steadily outside in shady positions which dry out somewhat in the summer but not to the extent of becoming parched and baked. They will do well half-sheltered by a small deciduous shrub.

F. meleagris 'Jupiter' is one of the richer-coloured cultivars of the snake's head fritillary, a good garden plant and always a popular choice.

Fritillaria meleagris
Linnaeus (1A) tri: Europe, including UK:
syn. *F. graminifolia.*

This plant is most commonly known as snake's head fritillary or lily but has many other names, including drooping tulip, death bell and leper's bell. It is first recorded as discovered by a chemist in a field 80km (50 miles) south of Paris, but it must have been well-known to country people from time immemorial. While it is known all over Europe, its centre of distribution is perhaps central France across to Switzerland. It is described as a native in British floras but in many places it is certainly an introduced plant. Though once recorded in 27 counties it is now known in only seven, with well-known colonies in Oxfordshire and Gloucestershire, where it grows in watermeadows outside Cricklade, not far from the source of the river Thames. It now has strict protected status, so it should not be collected as bulbs, seeds or flowers.

The species is extraordinarily uniform in most characteristics despite its number and distribution, flower colour being the obvious variable. The twin-scale bulb is large, somewhat squat and flat-topped. Mature bulbs can measure 5cm (2 inches) across, but ones half this size will produce flowers and will be accompanied by bulblets clustering around their bases. Growing in the grass the plants are easily lost with their grass-like foliage, which is usually bright green but sometimes duller. The leaves are alternate, sometimes measuring 13cm (5 inches) long, and sharply pointed. The large, square-shouldered pendant bells are solitary, opening mostly in mid-spring but with a few in early spring and some still showing colour in early summer; colouring varies from pure white to cream, pink, the standard mauve and dark purples, all except the whites being very clearly marked with lighter chequering. Inside the flowers are paler but splashed more with green and have shining green nectaries. Outside the nectaries are bony. The yellow anthers are half the length of the petals and the style at full length is deeply divided; the three-sided seedpods are smooth and wingless.

This splendid plant is the easiest of fritillaries and increases splendidly in moist spots. In very dry gardens it may tend to die out; most gardeners are willing to spend the few pence that is needed to purchase fresh bulbs to have the pleasure of seeing the flowers. It grows easily from seed and bulbs, but especially so if the soil is moist. Ideal conditions are where the plants are lightly shaded by grass or shrubs and the soil remains moist through the summer. In such places it may well naturalize itself by seeding freely. If seed is saved and sown in a cold frame and kept moist, the resulting plants will be blooming in their third year; those left to grow naturally will take double this time. It is a bulb that does much better in the ground than in pots.

F. m. alba White forms are gathered under this label. Like most albinos they tend to be rather less tall, at 13–20cm (5–8 inches), and perhaps a little less vigorous. There is little or no green veining in the clear white flowers, though there will be a small green patch over the nectaries. The petals are narrower and taper to a point.

F. m. 'Aphrodite' A white form with a hint of cream and with deep green veining inside and out, this veining starting at the large shining nectary and reaching down to the petal tips. It reaches 20–38cm (8–15 inches).

F.m. 'Artemis' Overall a grey flower because of a pervasive grey sheen that subdues the purple-red flower with pale tessellation. The height is 30–38cm (12–15 inches)

F. m. burnatii (Planchon). A dwarf Swiss plant only 8–10cm (3–4 inches) high with purple-grey flowers and short leaves.

F. m. 'Charon' One of the darkest of all – so dark is the purple colouring it is difficult to make out any of the chequered pattern. The height is 20–25cm (8–10 inches).

F. m. contorta First described over 100 years ago when it was discovered in a British population, then it disappeared for a decade only to reappear again. Presumably the original mutation has been duplicated more or less exactly. The tube-like flowers are brown, green and white and really rather meagre, held in a semi-pendant pose.

F. m. 'Jupiter' (Eckhart pre-1956). This is a beautiful selected clone with deep red flowers with lighter tessellation. It is 20–25cm (8–10 inches) high.

F. m. 'Orion' Of similar stature to 'Jupiter' and with rich violet-purple flowers with paler lilac chequering.

F. m. 'Pink Eveline' A welcome new variety, a vigorous plant 38–50cm (15–20 inches) tall with pale pink flowers shading to white and grey pink, neatly chequered on the outside. This wonderful plant should soon be widely available and may be the precursor of many fine new clones.

F. m. 'Poseidon' (Eckhart). A fine example of the standard colouring, a rich mauve with grey patterning. The height is 20–25cm (8–10 inches).

F. m. 'Saturnus' A fine selection, a clone with flowers a rich blood-red with paler lilac-red chequering. The height is 20–25cm (8–10 inches).

Fritillaria messanensis

(1C) Rafinesque: tri: Med., N. Africa:
syn. *F. algeriensis, F. illyrica, F. mauritanica,*
F. munbyi, F. neglecta, F. oranensis, F. sphaciottica.
This species grows widely around the Mediterranean countries and is the only fritillary to grow in North Africa. The bulb is formed of two oval scales joined in the centre by a pointed cone. The stem reaches 30–40cm (12–16 inches) with thin grey alternate leaves and a final whorl of 3–4 around the flowers, which are large hanging bells in pairs or threes, their exteriors being a mix of chequered brown, red and lime green with a green stripe down the centre of each petal, usually very conspicuous but varying in width. The petals form a close cloche hat with some light flanging at the rim. Inside they are paler with more green shading and with shining deep green patches around the nectaries; outside the nectaries are only lightly raised. The style is deeply divided and the capsules are broad, flat-topped, smooth and without wings.

While this is best suited to the Mediterranean climate it will grow well in bulb frames and may well thrive in gardens in southern Britain if given a dryish spot, perhaps in the lee of a shrub. Certainly it will grow well in a deep pot with some protection from hard frosts. Well-drained soil suits it, and the pots can be left outside in the summer to become almost completely dry. Plants come into bloom in late spring and increase to make an impressive clump in a relatively short space

F. messanensis is a Mediterranean species which is the only member of the genus to spread into North Africa. In cultivation it does well in bulb frames.

of time. It is very close to *F. graeca* and *F. involucrata*. In the wild it is to be found growing on grassy hillsides up to some 900m (3,000ft) in northern Greece, Crete, Sicily and North Africa.

F. m. atlantica (Maire) Rix, syn. *F. oranensis.* A smaller plant 15–20cm (6–8 inches) tall, from North Africa and with flowers of various colourings. Some are tubby blooms with wide-open brown to purple colouring with no patterns, others are similar to the type with a central light green stripe down each petal. The leaves are fewer, broader, lanceolate, and covered with a grey bloom.

This is a rare plant in cultivation, probably found in only a few collections.

F. m. gracilis (Ebel) Rix, syn. *F. neglecta*, *F. illyrica*. This plant from northern Albania and Macedonia is a smaller form growing 15–20cm (6–8 inches) high with flowers that may be light brown to red without patterning yet with a light yellow edge to the petals, but may be similar to the type with the central stripe changed to pale yellow and the insides being yellow or limy with deep round green nectaries. The leaves are fewer and narrower, a glossy grass green. This is in cultivation and in demand.

Fritillaria michailovskyi

(1C) Fomin: tri: Turkey.

This plant has become known worldwide although it was only rediscovered two decades ago on the Mathew and Tomlinson expedition to Turkey, having been originally found by Michailovski in 1904. It was micropropagated and is now one of the regulars in every garden centre. The bulb has two rounded scales and the short sturdy stems are 10–15cm (4–6 inches) high with a few leaves erect, alternately arranged and masking the stem; they are a pale lime green, broader than most and long with sharply pointed tips. The flowers of the typical plant are carried singly, very occasionally in pairs, and are large box-shaped pendant bells with recurving tips. Recently a number of plants have appeared carrying up to a massive seven blooms to a stem, maybe a matter of nursery selection. The two-thirds of the flower nearest the stem is a rich purple maroon and the lower third is a vivid contrast of gold, these two colours being repeated inside though just a little muted. The nectaries are purple to black, the styles are deeply divided and the seedpods are smooth and wingless.

The wild home of this species is the grassy alpine meadows of north-eastern Turkey up to 1,800m (6,000ft), especially around Lake Van and Kars. It is not a difficult plant, though it is slow to increase. Ideal soil will be a loose gritty loam which is very cold in winter and cool and dry in summer. The bulbs need the cold to encourage flowering; warm conditions tend to make the flowers malform and abort below soil level. It is impressive in a pot if conditions are right, but it is as much at home in a tub or trough where it will be in bloom late spring to early summer, later than potted plants under cover.

Fritillaria micrantha

(6D) Heller: tri: Calif: syn. *F. multiflora*, *F. parviflora*. Commonly known as the woodland brown bell, this plant is a close relative of *F. affinis*, *F. viridea* and *F. recurva*. Where it grows with the latter a natural hybrid occurs, *F. phaeanthera*. *F. micrantha* is a curious rather than a stunning fritillary. It has only recently entered cultivation in the UK. Seed is being sown and more will be known of the plant in another 5–10 years when experience has been gained. The bulb is small and solid, with numerous bulblets clustered around the base. The stem grows to 20–25cm (8–10 inches) with whorls of grey-green narrow leaves along the stem, arranged singly as they near the flowers, which are small and open hanging stars held within the leaf axils. Typical flower colour is mauve brown, darker towards the nectary, usually without any chequering. The nectaries are slightly raised on the outside and coloured purple inside; the style is deeply divided. The seed capsules have long wings on the four corners. The flowering season is late spring to early summer.

Hybrids with *F. recurva* may be reddish-brown and yellow or brown outside and orange to red inside. Crossed with *F. viridae*, the resultant hybrids have blooms that are green and brown outside but yellow inside. Hybrids with *F. affinis* are green-striped and chequered inside.

The wild plants are found growing in pine woodland at around 600m (2,000ft) along the west-facing slopes of the Sierra Nevada in eastern California. Summers here are dry and the winters cold, with wet snow. The soil is heavy clay with a covering of leafmould. If you are trying to raise these plants from seed it seems beneficial to keep the soil moist and free-draining for the first two years.

Fritillaria minima

(1D) Rix: tri: Turkey.

A rare plant in the wild and very scarce in cultivation – it is difficult to obtain even when you have found someone with a plant. The bulb is tiny, of two scales with a few small bulblets at the base. The stem is only 5cm (2 inches), with 5–7 relatively large broadly lanceolate leaves in polished green. They are alternately arranged

F. minima is a very small and tricky plant, a rarity both in its native habitat in the mountains of southern Turkey and in cultivation.

on the stem, which they tend to clasp. The solitary flowers, blooming in mid- to late spring, are narrow tubes facing outwards, yellow with green nectaries on the outside. Inside the nectaries are a dark green and the petals have green veining through the yellow. The styles are very thin and slightly reflexed, and the seed-pods are smooth and without wings.

This plant is closely allied to the larger *F. bithynica*. It is an endangered plant in the wild, and cultivation is not easy. It seems to need a stable environment, settled cold winters of around –1°C (30°F), a moist spring and a dry summer and autumn. The soil should be predominantly sharp grit with only a tithe of loam. In the wild it is a scarce Turkish native from the southern mountains around Lake Van at 2,700m (9,000ft).

Fritillaria minuta
(1D) Boissier & Noe: tri: Turkey:
syn. *F. carduchorum*.

Alphabetical listing coincidentally brings together two small species from the same location and both difficult ones in cultivation. However, unlike *F. minima*, *F. minuta* is readily available as it increases at quite a prodigious rate; it will soon produce numerous bulbs, though not necessarily numerous flowers. The bulb is small with many bulblets, but it is a mistake to dislodge too many as the plants seems to dislike it. The stem is some 10–15cm (4–6 inches), though some clones may reach 25cm (10 inches). It is a frequent characteristic for the large, lanceolate, deep glossy green leaves to fold in half and thus hang downwards. This is one of the leafier species, and often seems content to grow year in year out producing foliage and bulbs but never blooming. When the solitary flowers do appear they are horizontal or pendant, and either cone-shaped or longer and more tube-like. They may be apricot-brown or brick red, with an attractive dusty grey bloom; all are amber to yellow inside and with green nectaries. The style is as long as the petals and deeply trifid. Seed capsules seem difficult to achieve in cultivation, but in the wild they are smooth and wingless. Flowering is in mid-spring.

F. minuta grows wild in south-eastern Turkey around Lake Van at 1,500–2,000m (5,000–7,000ft). In a deep pot it multiplies well, but is chary of blooming. Outside it increases slowly and can grow strongly and try to produce a flower, but shortly after appearing this is usually aborted. The best regime seems to be a deep pot of grit

F. minuta is a leafy little plant which is much easier to grow than the rather similar elfin *F. minima*. For preference, give it a deep pot of grit and loam.

and loam, left outside during autumn and winter to enjoy the cold. In early spring, bring the pot under cover and provide warmth and moisture. In summer place the pot in shade and allow it to become virtually dry. This produces flowers at least every other year.

Fritillaria montana
(1C) Hoppe: tri: France to Greece: syn. *F. caussolesis*, *F. neglecta*, *F. nigra*, *F. orsiniana*, *F. racemosa*, *F. tenella*. Once gardeners realize how easy this plant is it could

F. minuta is easy to obtain as it increases prolifically. However, blooming is not so abundant and it may fail to flower for several years.

F. montana is found throughout several southern European countries and does very well in gardens. A regular bloomer, it will probably become very popular once its ease of cultivation is more widely appreciated.

become very popular. The bulb is relatively large with thick twin scales. It often produces stolons as thick white horizontal extensions for some 3cm (1¼ inches) or so with a small bulb at the end. The stem reaches 25cm (10 inches) tall with thin, sharp-pointed grey-green leaves, opposite at the base, alternate up the stems. One to three flowers are carried as short tubby bells, the rounded, almost egg-shaped petals irregularly coloured plum-purple to brown and chequered in green outside. Some clones have a green patch in the centre of each petal. Inside there is a pattern of green and

F. montana ruthenica, a rare plant in the wild in Bulgaria and Albania but not difficult in cultivation as long as it is given semi-shade and moist soil. It may grow to twice the height of the typical species.

chestnut tessellation with light green nectaries. The anthers are short and yellow; the style is deeply divided and the seed pods smooth and rounded.

This widespread species is found quite easily on steep slopes among tall grass or small bushes throughout southern France into northern Italy and through former Yugoslavia to northern Greece. It maintains its form with little variation. Surprisingly the plant tolerates the wetter conditions it finds in British gardens, even though the bulbs prefer drier summer soils. It is a regular bloomer and a steady rather than dramatic increaser. Flowering time is late spring to early summer. The plants thrive best in the lee of some small not too dominant shrub, perhaps *Berberis thunbergii* 'Aurea' or *Spiraea japonica* 'Gold Mound', a pleasing combination of yellow spring foliage and brown flowers.

F. m. meleagroides (Patrin ex. Schult), syn. *F. longifolia*. This form is very like the plant often known as *F. ruthenica*. It is found in remote damp meadows at 900m (3,000ft) in Bulgaria. The grey-green leaves are arranged alternately along 25cm (10 inch) stems. On top is a single flower, deep red but chequered purple outside, inside uniformly greenish. This is probably a relatively new plant in cultivation.

F. m. ruthenica (Wikstrom), syn. *F. heterophylla*, *F. minor*, *F. ruthenica*. A rare wild plant found in scattered locations in Bulgaria and Albania at 900m (3,000ft). It is much taller than the type at 25–50cm (10–20 inches), with grey-green opposite leaves and a whorl of three around the flowers. Most of the upper leaves have a little tendril tip which grasps any nearby vegetation. The flowers are like wide-open campanula bells with widely spaced petals, outside being a dark red with lemon-yellow edges. Inside there is a mix of brown, red and green. The style is deeply trifid and the seed pods are winged with dried tendrils at the base and top. Cultivation is not difficult if the soil is never allowed to dry out during the summer and the plants are given semi-shade.

Fritillaria obliqua
(1D) Ker-Gawler: tri–lobed: Greece.

Sadly this beautiful black fritillary is teetering on the brink of extinction, in cultivation and in its native woodland homes in Greece. This is even the more unfortunate in view of the fact that the plant can be grown relatively easily in the open garden. Two closely clasped scales make the bulbs, which produce stems 15–20cm (6–8 inches) tall with a few broad leaves. They alternate on the lower half of the stem and are a deep grey-green. The flowers are normally solitary but there can be a cluster of up to eight on occasions; only 2cm long and 3cm wide (¾ x 1¼ inches), they make their impact by their glossy blackness, a delicate sheen that can be spoilt by careless fingers. On the inside the somewhat incurved petals are midnight black. The scent is described by some as sweet and others as pungent. Deeply pitted nectaries are at the base of the style, which is only lightly divided. The seed pods are smooth and rounded.

F. obliqua comes from the chalky mountain slopes around Athens, Greece, but few plants still persist in the wild. It blooms in late spring and in British gardens prefers a cool, sharply drained soil with some summer shade. This species and F. tuntasia can be easily confused, although the styles are different. Other major differences include the absence of grey bloom on the leaves of F. tuntasia, its stouter, taller stems up to 45cm (18 inches) high and its being more difficult to grow than F. obliqua.

Fritillaria olgae
(1B) Vedensky: tri: Asia Minor.

This plant is closely related to F. regelii, but as neither species is thought to be in cultivation little is known of their requirements. The stem grows to 60cm (24 inches) with rich green slender to ovate leaves held opposite each other and twisted with a short tendril tip. The broad, wide-open, pendant flowers are grouped in a bunch of 5–8, each chequered purple and green with a deep purple tip to the petals. The style is deeply divided and the capsule smooth and wingless.

F. olgae is a native of northern Iran and Turkmenistan. It appears to grow in well-drained spots which do not dry out in the summer. Active root growth seems to start with the coming of winter and the plant comes into bloom at the end of the winter or very early spring.

Fritillaria olivieri
(1C) Baker: tri: Iran.

This is a rare species, although every 2–3 years collected seed is offered in the lists of the more specialist societies. It germinates quickly from seed and grows well to produce clumps of flowering plants quite quickly. Two tightly joined scales make the main bulb, which has many bulblets around the base. The stem reaches 30–38cm (12–15 inches), with broad dull green basal leaves; those above are narrower and at the top there is a whorl of three held over the flowers. These are distinctively marked with a green stripe down the centre of each petal; to the sides the colouring is a rusty brown and red chequered pattern. Single square-shouldered bells are recurved to allow a glimpse of the red and green striped tips, beyond which the stripe disappears and the surface is a mix of red and green with a proportionately large nectary area patch of darker green. The anthers are yellow and the style only slightly divided.

This splendid plant has affinities to F. hermonis of the F. crassifolia group. It belongs to the damp grassy areas of western Iran at some 3,000m (10,000ft) in the Zagros mountains and is usually found in red sandy turf not far from water. It is not a particularly difficult plant when grown in a deep pot, where it increases easily and flowers from mid- to late spring. Give protection from late frosts and a summer rest period.

Fritillaria pallidiflora
(1A) Schrenk: tri: Asia.

This was discovered by botanist and plantsman Eduard Von-Regel, President of the Russian Horticultural Society, and sold from his nursery catalogues through the period of 1885–1916. It was known to be hardy in

British gardens then, but was only planted sparingly as the bulbs were very expensive. After World War II a number of bulbs were reintroduced and it did well in the open in gardens of the southern counties. It achieved a huge rate of increase but failed to become popular and drifted out of the catalogues. In western China, where this species is used for medicinal purposes, it is grown in ridges rather like potatoes. Bulbs are grown in Holland for gardeners, but the species has still to achieve the popularity it deserves.

Two or three thick fleshy scales joined at the base make sizeable bulbs; the stems are strong and stout, 20–45cm (8–18 inches) tall, with thick fleshy grey-green leaves, broad to ovate at the base with the upper ones lanceolate. The large, pendant, square-topped bell flowers vary from a rich butter to a lemon shade on the outside with the insides primrose lightly speckled with light red pepper; there may be half a dozen. On the inside the nectary is clearly indented, on the outside it is raised, covered with a green sheen on both surfaces. The trifid style protrudes beyond the anthers and the seed pods have wide wings rather similar to those of *F. imperialis*.

F. pallidiflora hails from central Asia. In the wild it is found in moist peaty meadows which never dry out. This must be emulated in the garden, and it should certainly not suffer from the summer drought that many species relish. It may be a little slow to increase for a year or two after planting but thereafter should increase steadily and be one of the most regular early summer bloomers. It will survive winter temperatures of –10°C (14°F).

F. p. lixianensis (Y. K. Yang). From Szechuan province in China, this closely related purple-flowered plant could be a separate species. It is probably not at present in cultivation.

F. p. uniflora This is somewhat shorter than the type at 15–20cm (6–8 inches) and with solitary flowers. It is probably not in cultivation.

Fritillaria persica
(3) Linnaeus: e: Cyprus, Turkey, Iran, Syria.
On four occasions this species has been taken out of the *Fritillaria* genus. It is certainly different, perhaps the most distinct of the genus. The bulb is large, second only in size to *F. imperialis*, and is quite different in form, being oval, almost egg-shaped, somewhat pointed and

with two scales welded together to make the bulb, one scale being larger than the other. Bulbs can be up to 10–13cm (4–5 inches) long. The stem can be up to 1m (3¼ft) tall; in sheltered spots by shrubs these plants should be strong enough on their own but it does no harm to insert a cane when they begin to emerge and tie the stems for safety. Numerous lanceolate leaves are produced on the stem, both stem and foliage being a pleasing grey rather than green, a grey that can be easily spoilt by handling or brushing against other stems. The flowerhead can measure 25cm (10 inches) long, with up to 30 small conical pendant bells. These are a deep plum-purple with a very fine grey-plum bloom. The lowest flowers open first in early spring but they last well so that the plant is a focus of attention for several weeks, the last flowers opening towards the end of spring. Inside the flowers are usually a shining purple made more impressive by the contrasting bright yellow anthers. The nectaries are highly raised outside and inside are indented and grass-green. Many flowers lack styles, but when present they are short, slender and entire. Possibly some 10 per cent of the flowers will produce seed pods. These are short, thin and faintly winged, with only a light yield of seed.

In the wild the species is most often found growing among rocks and scrub on hillsides up to around 2,100m (7,000ft), especially in Cyprus, Turkey, Iran and Syria. It is hardy in that it can be grown perfectly well outside in the south of the UK but further north its hardiness status is more problematical. Wherever it is grown the main problem is late frosts; given the slightest encouragement in the second half of the winter the bulbs stir into growth and by the end of the winter the plants can be in full leaf and ready to bloom in early to mid-spring. It is sensible to cover the ground above the plants with loose waste, dried fern, bracken or other open material that will fend off the worst of the frost and protect the young shoots. Planted with heathers to the front and rather larger shrubs behind, they will do well enough. This species likes well-drained soils rich in compost, an open-textured mix that should not be allowed to dry out even in the summer. The bulbs can increase very pleasingly if left undisturbed; seed will produce plenty of plants with healthy foliage but they may take five years to reach flowering size.

F. p. 'Adiyaman' Although the variety name is often used in catalogues the true plant is difficult to acquire. It is a shorter form, some 60cm (24 inches) tall, named after the town in southern Turkey where it was discovered. The shorter stems make it a much easier plant to manage in the garden; most gardeners would choose it as the preferred form. The flowers are darker and more closely set. The whole effect is more compact; an exotic but sturdy plant.

F. p. alba This is a rare and beautiful plant in cultivation though not plentiful. Even with an expensive price tag it is worth searching out. Stems 75cm (30 inches) tall carry creamy-white bells covered in a grey bloom, a quite entrancing effect.

F. p. libanotica This is often listed as a synonym of *F. persica*; however, the true variety has greenish-yellow flowers and grows at 1,200m (4,000) in the Lebanon.

Fritillaria phaeanthera

(6D) Eastwood: tri: Calif.: syn. *F. eastwoodiae*.
This is a natural hybrid between *F. micrantha* and *F. recurva*. There is dissension among botanists as to whether it should be called *F. phaeanthera* or *F. eastwoodiae*; it is listed here under the former name as this is how it appears in the majority of bulb reference books. The bulb is rounded with a pointed centre and covered in rice grain bulblets. The stem is about 30cm (12 inches) tall with small, thin, grey-green leaves either held in whorls or arranged alternately along the slender stem. The flowers are larger and more attractive than those of the slightly dowdy *F. micrantha*, 2cm (¾ inches) across, cone or wider bell-shaped with recurving petals. Colouring may be predominantly orange, yellow or brown, with no chequered pattern but merely a blend of the three colours. Up to seven flowers are carried on a stem. The style and yellow anthers protrude beyond the petals, the former being divided with the three parts curling backwards. The flowering period is around mid-spring. The seed pods have three dried wings.

This hybrid plant is found in the Sierra Nevada foothills of California. In the garden it can be temperamental; it needs winter protection and is best grown in a deep potful of gritty loam that is allowed to dry out almost completely in summer. To protect it from spring frosts it is best kept in a cool greenhouse or similar shelter during the spring.

F. latifolia aurea × F. pinardii, an intermediate hybrid with flowers that are larger than those of *F. pinardii*. As is the case with the majority of hybrids, it is perhaps a stronger plant than either of its parents.

Fritillaria pinardii

(1D) Boissier: e: Turkey:
syn. *F. alpina, F. fleischeri, F. syriaca*.
This is a variable little plant from the *F. bithynica* group. There are several forms and a series of hybrids between it and *F. bithynica* and *F. armena*. The large bulb has a number of bulblets attached to the base and slender stoloniferous shoots spreading sideways and ending with tiny bulbs. The stem is usually 5–10cm (2–4 inches) only, but there are some unusual taller forms that might

F. pinardii, a neat, slender plant from Turkey that grows well in gritty soil in the open garden or in pots. There are a number of colour forms, though none have as yet been given official cultivar names.

reach up to 20cm (8 inches). The alternate dark green leaves are narrow but the basal two are somewhat broader. Typically the solitary flowers are yellow and brown, but this may vary to become yellow with stripes of brown and purple or completely brown with no other markings. Occasional strong bulbs will produce two or three flowers, tube-like bells with petals recurved, the outer three more so than the inner set. The inner surfaces are either purple or yellow with greenish nectaries, yellow anthers and entire styles.

This is one of the most widespread species in Turkey, growing throughout the mountains at 1,200–2,100m (4–7,000ft). The dark forms come from the triangle formed by south-eastern Turkey, Lake Van, Malatya and Syria, while the yellow and brown forms are found in north-eastern Turkey up towards the Black Sea. It is not difficult to grow and will bloom in late spring in a warm corner of the rock garden or in a trough, though some forms are more suitable for growing under glass. They should be kept cool in the winter and moist during the spring, with shade and little moisture through the summer. Soil is the usual loam and grit.

There is a temptation to give particular colour forms fancy cultivar names, though there are currently no official ones. At present you may be able to run to earth these selected ones: a giant 25cm (10 inches) kind often with three flowers, an orange-brown one with a golden-yellow centre, a lime-yellow with purple-brown margins and a chocolate-purple with lime-yellow petal edges. These may appear at shows, when owners will be able to give their sources.

F. p. kittaniae This is an up-and-coming show plant like the typical species except that the petals are reddish-brown with a central green stripe and the outer three are strongly recurving, the inner three only slightly so.

Fritillaria pluriflora
(6F) Baker: e: lobed: Calif.

This is a wonderful species but it can be an achievement to keep the plant from one season to the next and there is no guarantee of flowers. The bulb is a little collection of scales, stretching from a flat bottom covered in numerous tiny rice grain bulblets. The stem rises to 23–30cm (9–12 inches) with a large number of long, lanceolate, fleshy or waxy leaves clustered around the

base. A few upright thin leaves clasp the stem up to and around the flowers. These almost look like a wild gladiolus or pink schizostylis gathered on a short thick flowering spike, as many as 5–12 held horizontally. They are open, pale pink to rich rose-red and not patterned, though they have some darker shading around the outside of the nectaries. Inside the petals are slightly lighter with a central deeper pink vein running down towards the rich pink nectaries. The anthers are short and yellow, and the style is entire but with a suggestion of lobing. It appears to be a reluctant seeder – in the wild there may be broad, smooth, flat-topped seed pods but even these may contain few viable seeds. In cultivation seed pods are extremely rare.

This species needs the protection of an alpine house or greenhouse to protect it from frost; it will not stand much more than a short period at –3°C (27°F). Ideal soil for it will be limy, wet and almost like modelling clay in winter, drying out in summer like the adobe soils of its native areas which bake hard as brick. The bulb in the wild will be deep and insulated; in cultivation it needs a large pot so that it can be planted 20cm (8 inches) deep. It can take 2–3 years for a bulb to settle down and produce a flower in early summer. When flowers fade they may be nipped off to circumvent the unlikely production of seed pods which may drain the bulb of energy that would be better used for further flower production.

In the wild *F. pluriflora* is becoming rare, as cattle eat the flowers before they can open and reproduce. A few colonies are to be found on the valley floors at low altitudes up to 600m (2,000ft) on grazing land of the Sierra Nevada, California. It is essential to find foolproof ways of reproducing this plant and providing it with some wild sanctuary before its endangered status becomes even more critical.

F. p. alba Although it is in cultivation, this plant is one of the rarest of all. It has a taller stem, bearing fewer flowers; these are pendant and with more incurved petals, each pure white.

F. pinardii is a widespread and varied species which in the wild is usually found in mountainous areas. The darker forms come from south-eastern Turkey, while the yellow and brown forms grow in the north-east of the country up towards the Black Sea.

Fritillaria pontica
(1C) Wahlenberg: tri: Balkans and Turkey:
syn. *F. olympica.*

This is a plant for lovers of green flowers, an easy, hardy species that ought not to be overlooked – and indeed should be looked at from underneath, as there are six black eyes staring from the backs of the petals. The bulb is formed of two scales that look as if they are held together by the central shoot. From one scale there will be a stolon hooked over the top. The stem grows to 20–38cm (8–15 inches) with broad, grey, lanceolate, alternate leaves along the sturdy stem. At the top there is a whorl of three leaves sitting over the 2–3 flowers. While a deep grey-green on the outside, inside the green is shaded and veined brown and this brown theme extends to a band running around the petal edges. Outside the nectaries are smooth with no colour variation, inside they are dramatically circled in black. The anthers are yellow and the style is clearly trifid. Long thin seed pods with dry wings are freely produced and contain plenty of seed. Flowering period is mid-spring.

Bulbs multiply quickly in leafy loam soils which are kept moist during the summer and both cool and moist through the winter. The plant benefits from some shade, especially when in bloom otherwise the flowers quickly wilt and fall. *F. pontica* is closely allied to *F. graeca*; in the wild they can be found growing together. Its native habitat is the mountains of Albania across to Bulgaria, northern Greece and western Turkey, climbing to 2,100m (7,000ft).

F. p. substipelata (Candorgy). Found on the island of Lésvos, Greece, this differs in having thinner leaves and taller stems. The elongated bells maintain the typical green but are covered in a silvery-grey bloom on the outside. Inside the petals each have a deep red patch at the petal tips. While not yet listed in bulb catalogues, it is a not infrequent name in seedlists. It is worth finding as it is a distinctive character, easy enough to grow in moist soils.

Fritillaria pudica
(6E) Sprengel: e: N. America.

Commonly known as Johnny-jump-up or little yellow bell, this is the most popular of fritillaries among growers of alpines. Hardy outside in trough or scree gardens, it is also eye-catching in a pot. The bulb is only as big as a pea, solid and with numerous pinhead-size bulblets at the base. The reddish-green stem reaches 7–13cm (3–5 inches), carrying a few thin, dark green, sword-shaped leaves twisted and lunging upwards, but kept so close to the stems as to obscure them almost completely. The 1–3 hanging flowers are usually golden-yellow but with its wide distribution there are a number of colour variants. There is no shading or tessellation on the petals, the only normal variation being the green of the nectaries. The wingless seedpods are rounded.

F. pudica is a well-defined species, an unusual American one in that it has an entire style like most European species. It comes from the cold rocky mountains of northwest North America, where it is found growing in short grass or rocky screes up to some 1,800m (6,000ft). In British gardens it will tolerate wet winters provided the soil is sharply drained. In a warm corner of a rock, scree or trough garden it will bloom from late spring to early summer. It has been recommended as one of the best for growing in pots, where the bulbs increase quickly. Allow them to become almost completely dry in summer.

While this is such a well-defined species, not hybridizing in the wild, it does produce a series of colour forms, perhaps as many as 10 distinct ones. Most of these are to be found named after the district where they were discovered. Colourings are a combination of orange, yellow, green and brown shades. They vary too in height and the flower size.

F. p. 'Richard Britain' This selection has become very popular. The sterile flowers are much larger than the type and are a very bright golden yellow inside and out.

Fritillaria purdyi
(6B) Eastwood: tri: Calif.

A really beautiful species, this is one that is not too difficult to grow. The bulb has a number of fleshy scales but rarely any bulblets at the base. The stem reaches 13–18cm (5–7 inches) with a collection of fleshy, upright and twisted leaves near the soil. The stem is then bare up to the level of the flowers, where there are 1–2 thin leaves with the blooms. The 1–5 thick waxen flowers may be pendant or swung somewhat

F. pudica 'Richard Britain' is one of the brightest forms of the species and is also one of the less awkward of the American kinds in cultivation. It is consequently a very popular plant.

outward-facing, the shiny petals just managing to touch each other. Outside they are white or green, splashed or streaked with brown or red. Inside the green is splashed with brown in the centre while the petal margins are a creamy white. Some clones may be a mix of green and white on the outside with only a few brown spots inside. The nectaries are prominently raised on the outside, indented on the inside and a deep green or brown. The style is deeply divided and short, with the orange or yellow anthers tucked below; the seed pods are winged and still retain the wasted style.

This plant is seen at its best in the alpine house, where it will bloom mid- to late spring. It is not difficult in a deep pot with heavy loam or clay soil which should be allowed to dry out almost completely in summer. *F. purdyi* grows in stony clay screes and pine woodland in northern California on the west-facing coastal foothills but also higher, up to 2,100m (7,000ft). It is listed in many catalogues but stock is still shorter than the demand.

Fritillaria pyrenaica
(1C) Linnaeus: tri: Pyrenees:
syn. *F. aquitanica, F. lurida, F. nervosa, F. umbellata.*

This is a plant which will grow well in several different garden situations and is not fussy about the weather. It has acquired a reputation for being evil-smelling, but that is unjust – it is slightly foxy but less so than the crown imperials. The bulb is twin-scaled, with a sturdy stem rising 25–45 cm (10–18 inches); the alternate leaves are erect and grass-like, green with occasionally some light grey dusting. The beautiful flowers are solitary or very occasionally in pairs, the hanging bells being deeply recurved at the petal tips, a stylish shape. Outside they can be chequered red and brown with a yellow-green stripe or this lime colour can be reduced to the chequered pattern within the red and brown background. Some forms look completely brown, but on closer inspection some tessellation can be seen. Inside the petals are more stable, the predominant colour being yellow with a light brown chequering towards the nectary, which penetrates deeply and is lime green. On the outside the nectary forms a highly raised hump which runs down towards the petal centres. The style is either standard trifid or on occasion can be divided into 5–8 divisions. The seed pods are smooth and without wings.

This species will flower within three years from seed, one of the fastest of all; if any fail to make it in three they should certainly flower in the fourth. Bulbs are readily available from bulb nurserymen, and will grow easily outside under a small shrub in full sun, flowering from late spring to early summer. In the Pyrenees this plant is found growing in isolated patches of grassy, stony slopes. It is becoming scarce on the French side but on the Spanish side it can be found growing freely with *F. lusitanica.*

F. p. lutea syn. *F. p.* 'Old Gold', *F. p. lutescens.* This is a highly prized version for the specialist collection. It has similar foliage to the type but may have up to four flowers, golden-yellow or lime-green. The nectaries are green on the outside with darker veining along the raised humps; on the inside the green is restricted to the nectary itself. It is more usual for seed to be offered rather than bulbs. This seed will give mixed results – a further generation may be necessary to get the better yellow forms.

Fritillaria raddeana
(2) Regel: e–lobed: Asia, Asia Minor:
syn. *F. askhabadensis.*

Clearly a close relative of *F. imperialis*, this plant was first listed commercially in 1909 but is now rarely offered, although you can find it in some lists and seed is available. It is reputed to be always without the foxy crown imperial scent. The bulb is large, rounded and formed of two closely clasped scales; the stem is robust although slender, 50–75cm (20–30 inches) tall with broad, glossy dark green, lanceolate leaves which are arranged alternately up the stem to within 15cm (6 inches) of the flowers, a distinct difference from *F. imperialis.* The 6–12 flowers, borne mid- to late spring, sit over this short bare segment of stem with a crown of dull narrow leaves above. Each star-shaped pendant bloom has a slender pedicle 5cm (2 inches) long held horizontally from the stem; the petals overlap a little, all being painted a primrose yellow with a light veining in green. The nectaries are raised on the outside as rounded bumps; inside they are a deep green with a white eye. The style, which is not always present, protrudes clearly and is entire or lightly lobed. The seed pods are winged, short and fat and have a perhaps undeserved reputation of being unlikely to set seed.

The species is widespread in the wild on low screes, cliff crevices and hillsides up to 600m (2,000ft). It ranges through central Asia, especially in Afghanistan, into north-eastern Iran and south-eastern Turkey. Articles written in the 1930–40s describe this as an easy plant in open soil in full sun and it is still one of the easiest outdoor fritillaries.

Fritillaria recurva
(6D) Bentham: tri: N. America.

This is the only red American species. The bulb is small and composed of a number of tiny scales forming a flat bulb with numerous bulblets underneath. The slender stem rises high, some 44–60cm (16–24 inches), with 1–3 whorls of grey-green linear leaves and occasionally another one under the flowers, of which there are 1–6 tube-shaped pendant widely spaced bells, each with distinctly recurved petal tips, borne in early summer. Colouring is usually a chequered pattern of scarlet, deeper red and gold. Inside the petals have an extensive tessellated pattern of yellow with the nectaries also yellow or green. These are indented inside and raised on the outside. The divided style curls back on itself and the seed pod has small, flimsy wings. In the USA the flowers are highly attractive to humming birds. While widely available it has not proved that easy to grow in the UK and may not last for more than two years outside in the north. However, it grows reasonably well in a deep pot with a mixture of leafmould and loam. The winter should be cold and moist, the summer shady and dry without being baked. In the wild it can expect frequent frosty winters with snow during the spring. It is native to Oregon and California at altitudes up to 2,000m (6,500ft).

F. r. coccinea (Greene). This form is only found in the San Francisco Bay area of California at low altitudes, the flowers being even more recurved and larger than the type with only a small amount of yellow chequering. The red is darker and almost covers the whole of the petals.

F. r. gentneri A form from southern Oregon, this plant has larger flowers with wide mouths and no recurving. The petals are dark wine red and with little or no yellow markings.

Fritillaria regelii
(1B) A. Losina: tri: Kyrgyzstan, Kazakhstan

This is one of the desirable species beyond the reach of all but a few growers treasuring plants raised from material introduced some years ago. However, one day more seed pods will be collected and it is to be hoped that these will give rise to populations that may help to maintain it and perhaps avert the threat to its existence in the wild. It comes from the Tien Shan range of mountains in Kyrgyzstan and Kazakhstan. The stem is 25cm (10 inches) tall with thin pointed green leaves, alternately arranged up the stem to the flowers, above which there is a crown of grassy leaves. The flowers appear in mid-spring, emerging from the leaf axils; there are 1–5 pendulous blooms in typical fritillary colours, chequered brown, lime-yellow and purple with a grey bloom over all the outside. The nectary is raised outside and green inside.

Fritillaria reuteri
(1C) Boissier: tri: Iran.

This is very similar to *F. michailovskyi* except that it is taller, with more but shorter flowers. The bulb is small and twin-scaled, producing a stem which reaches 18–25cm (7–10 inches) with many long lanceolate leaves at the base and a few thin bract-like ones scattered along the stem and around the flowers. These mid-spring blooms are squat, wide, rich maroon to red bells with open faces swung up horizontally and vivid yellow margins. The nectaries are humped outside with no colour distinction and the style is deeply divided.

This rare species is found in the Zagros mountains of Iran on grassy loamy slopes. There a few plants in cultivation. It is best in an alpine house given a cold moist winter, a cool wet spring and a cool wet summer – not the norm for the genus.

Fritillaria rhodia
(1D) A. Hansen: e: Rhodes, Turkey.

This is very similar to, and is often listed with, *F. bithynica*. It is restricted to low ground below 300m (1,000ft) on the south-western Turkish coastline and the island of Rhodes, where it was discovered fairly recently. The twin-scaled bulb is rounded. Stems 25–30cm (8–10 inches) high are accompanied by narrow grass-like leaves with pointed tips; 1–3 narrow early-spring

flowers are greenish yellow on their exteriors. Inside there is a richer golden colour with green nectaries. It is reported as teetering on the brink of extinction in the wild and is apparently not in cultivation.

Fritillaria rhodokanakis
(1C) Orphanides ex Baker: tri: Greece:
syn. *F. argolica, F. macrandra.*
This endangered little plant grows on limestone hillsides at 450m (1,500ft) on the tiny island of Idhra at the southernmost tip of Greece. The broad green leaves of lanceolate form are arranged alternately; they become narrower up the 15cm (6 inch) stem. The pendant flowers have recurved petal tips, with the top half of the flower painted maroon to purple, the lower half pale yellow. They open in mid-spring. The nectaries are humped outside and the style is deeply divided.

Fritillaria sewerzowii
(5) Regel 1868: e: S. Russia, Asia.
This distinct plant has moved in and out of the fritillary genus more than once after examinations by various botanists; it is now generally accepted to be the sole member of a separate genus, *Korolkowia sewerzowii.* Because it has so many characteristics in common with fritillaries it is given space here among its nearest relatives. It has a large bulb composed mainly of one massive scale with a central hole left by last season's stem. The new stem grows to 25–40cm (10–16 inches) with opposite elliptical leaves at the base and much thinner linear alternate ones along the stem. There are narrow leaves squatting among and around the flowers. All the foliage is grey. The flowers are slender tubes that flare outwards halfway along the petals, making a feature of the black anthers in the centre. There can be up to 15, all held in the leaf axils, the number depending upon the strength of the bulb. Colours vary from the usual green and brown outside and pure green inside to the exceptional purple and green clones. The nectaries are quite noticeable as long ridges outside and inside, painted a mix of purple and chocolate. If present, the style is entire, fat and set back on the petal bases.

F. reuteri is an Iranian species that is close to *F. michailovskyi* but usually much taller, with more numerous but shorter flowers. It is rare both in the wild in the Zagros mountains and in cultivation.

The foliage of a non-flowering plant of *F. sewerzowii*, a species that in the wild grows in scree conditions on hillsides but is surprisingly easy to cultivate.

In the wild the species is thinly spread over a wide area from Kyrgyzstan, Kazakhstan, Afghanistan, northern Pakistan, Kashmir and well into China. Its usual haunts are the loose screes or near scree-like conditions of hillsides up to around 1,800m (6,000ft).

In cultivation *F. sewerzowii* has proved to be surprisingly easy in pots or in the bulb frame. It can certainly withstand a few degrees of frost and varying water conditions during the winter and spring, but it is a good idea to keep the bulbs dryish during the summer. As the foliage can start to poke through in midwinter it is wise to give protection then; the flowers form from early to mid-spring.

Fritillaria sibthorpiana
(1D) (Smith) Baker: e: Turkey.

This is a recently discovered species close to *F. pinardii*. The orthodox twin-scaled bulb produces a stem 10–15cm (4–6 inches) tall with two leaves, a single basal one that is oval veering to lanceolate and a thin grassy one halfway up the stem; each is covered with a grey bloom. The solitary late-spring flower is pure gold both inside and out without any variation even around the nectaries. The outer three petals point outwards

F. sewerzowii is a distinct plant that is now more usually botanically classified as the solitary member of a separate genus, *Korolkowia sewerzowii*.

and are slightly recurved, while the inner set are held straight and so hide the anthers and style. The nectaries are smooth and styles are thick and entire.

This is a delightful fritillary from the south-western Mulga province of Turkey, where it is restricted to moist, lime woodlands at around 300m (1,000ft). Among the usual squat forms there may be specimens of the much taller form which can reach a height of 20cm (8 inches). In cultivation it is more readily available as seed than bulbs but is still scarce; seed takes 4–5 years to reach flowering size so that it will not be easily available quickly unless it is micropropagated. While slow to increase in a pot, it is not outstandingly difficult to cultivate.

Fritillaria stenanthera
(4) Regel: e: Asia.

This is an unusual fritillary from central Asia, with flowers rather widely opened and close to horizontally posed. A small round bulb of two scales produces a stem of 15–25cm (6–10 inches) tall with the lowest basal leaf clasping and enclosing the lower stem; other low leaves are narrower and more erect, while those produced with the flowers are narrow and point upwards. The foliage is a uniform dark shining green which takes on a reddish tinge with age. Predominantly palish-pink flowers have a large circle of purple around the nectaries, the whole being a dark-centred star. The equal nectaries are prominent, characterizing the species by being deeply humped, dark purple to black and almost 1cm (¼ inch) long. Most flowers are without styles but when present they are entire.

F. stenanthera can be grown outside in the UK but the flowers will probably be damaged by the spring frosts. The first leaves begin to emerge in late winter for flowering in early spring; for this reason alone the plant is best protected in an alpine house or cold greenhouse, grown in rich moist soil during the spring and then given a dry summer. It should also do well in a bulb frame that can offer frost protection in the second half of the winter and early spring. Neither seeds nor bulbs are difficult to grow but the bulbs always seem in short supply. It is native to Central Asia, in Uzbekistan and Afghanistan across to northern Iran, its most important locations being around Tashkent and Chimgan, where it is found growing on grassy hillsides near melting snow at 1,200–1,800m (4,000–6,000ft).

Fritillaria straussii
(1C) Bornmuller: tri: Turkey, Iran.

A plant similar to *F. crassifolia* though larger, rarely offered at present. A quite large, round, rather squat bulb of two tight scales produces the stout stem of 8–13cm (3–5 inches). It is a rather leafy plant with glossy large lanceolate leaves held in quite tightly packed whorls, the leaves twisting like an aeroplane propeller. One or two flowers open to face outwards with petals quite widely spaced and with very little or no recurving, coloured in shades of dark brown chequered green, sometimes only lightly but more pronounced in some clones. With maturity the colour usually becomes closer to dark maroon and the petals begin to recurve. Outside the nectaries are smooth with no colour change; inside they are green. The style is trifid and the seed pods are smooth. Flowering is usually mid-spring.

This plant needs very gritty open soil, probably in a bulb frame. In the wild it is found in western Turkey and northern Iran in loose scree at levels around 1,500–2,100m (5,000–7,000ft).

Fritillaria striata
(6F) Eastwood: tri: N. America.

Few fritillaries are as deliciously fragrant as *F. striata*. The bulb of this plant is a solid disc with a few rice grains at the base. A stem of 20–30cm (8–12 inches) high has a few clustered basal leaves reaching up with pointed tips and often with a twist in their length; the stem is then clear of foliage until the delightfully formed pendant bell-shaped flowers, where there may be 1–2 very narrow leaf bracts pointing up. The recurved petals are creamy white or white lightly blushed pink, though inside they are usually clearly striped pink. Individuals may be rather more richly coloured, a dark pink similar to its relative *F. pluriflora*. The nectaries of the two species are quite different, those of *F. plurifolia* being straight while those of *F. striata* are oval or elliptical. Outside the raised nectaries are darker pink, inside they are a creamy green. The style is deeply divided and the seed pods are not winged. The flowers open in mid-spring.

From time to time this is offered in the form of seed; bulbs are rarely listed. It is likely to remain one of the more difficult of American species to grow, being a plant of the adobe clays of the Greenhorn Mountains in

Tulane and Kern counties of California at around 600m (1,800ft) – a lime clay that is wet in winter but can bake hard as bricks in the summer.

Fritillaria stribrnyi
(1D) Velen: e: Balkans, Turkey.

Little is known about this endangered plant, one of a number of species that have been brought into cultivation but have not survived very long. The twin-scaled bulbs increase very slowly. The stem reaches 15–25cm (6–10 inches) with grey-green, linear, alternate leaves and with a whorl of three over the 1–3 flowers. These mid-spring blooms are tube-shaped, in tones of either pure purple or mixed with green but all covered with a dusty grey bloom. Inside they are shades of lime green. The long style is entire, and the broad seed pods have six wings.

The wild plant can go unnoticed in the grass and scrub at around 450m (1,500ft) in western Turkey and across to southern Bulgaria. It is closely related to *F. bithynica*.

Fritillaria thunbergii
(1B) Miquel: tri: Asia:
syn. *F. altaica, F. collincola, F. leucantha, F. verticillata.*

This is a species with tendril-tipped leaves that give it the appearance of being a climber. The bulb is twin-scaled and elongated, producing a stem 60–75cm (24–30 inches) tall with numerous leaves, bright green and held mostly in whorls, the lowest leaves being broadly lanceolate, the upper ones much thinner and with tendrils such as those of peas at the tips. In the wild these are used to hold the plants steady among the long grasses. Up to six flowers are produced from the upper leaf axils, each 2.5cm (1 inch) long, usually pendant but often upward-facing in the long grass. They are creamy white with green veining on the outside, chequered brown inside. The nectaries are green inside and out. The style is divided and the seed pods are winged and set at an angle to the stem, with flat tops and accompanying dried tendrils.

In Japan and China this plant is cultivated in ridges and sold in markets as a cough medicine. The bulbs multiply quickly, especially if they are planted near the soil surface, and over the last decade some bulbs that

F. thunbergii, a tendril-tipped Japanese and Chinese species which will grip shrubs and climbs if given support.

reproduce quickly but do not bloom are said to have found their way on to the European market. This rumour has hindered the cultivation of this species, but the authors have never found bulbs that are unwilling to bloom in moist peaty soils provided they are planted as deep as 25–30cm (10–12 inches) and then left undisturbed and starved. The stems and flowers need some support while they are blooming in the mid to late spring. In the wild *F. thunbergii* is widespread, growing from Uzbekistan across into China and Tibet. It is widely grown in Japan as a cultivated species but also as an introduced plant that has naturalized.

F. t. dagana (Turczaninov). Although it is not known in cultivation this is described as a single-flowered kind with slender stems and each petal of the flower chequered brown and purple.

F. t. maximowiczii (Freeyn). This is a large single-flowered form in purple with yellow chequering. It has been collected from eastern Siberia and is now held in a number of private botanical collections.

F. t. ussuriensis (Maximowicz). Thin stems up to 30cm (12 inches) high carry purple and chocolate flowers. It is unique in the manner in which it holds its seed pods; there is a 4cm (1½ inch) horizontal pedicle from the main stem with the bent pods held at 90°. Bulbs have been collected from the forests of Siberia.

Fritillaria tubiformis
(1A) Grenier & Godron: lobed: France:
syn. *F. delphinhensis.*

It is easy to confuse this species with *F. latifolia*, though it is usually taller with grey-green leaves and seems to grow more easily. The twin-scaled bulbs, which are slow to increase, produce stems 10–20cm (4–8 inches) high with a broad low leaf and a few much more slender ones up the stem towards the solitary flower, where three leaves are held together pointing upwards. The flowers are globular, red peppered purple with a grey bloom on the outside. This colour is by no means fixed, some forms being close to creamy white outside. The density of bloom is also variable, some being lightly covered while the colour of others is masked by a thick layer. The usual interior coloration is a purple to red peppered yellow, but some forms can be peppered green or white; some may be heavily

F. tubiformis has disproportionately large blooms carried on quite short stems. The colouring of this species from the southern French Alps is variable.

covered with a creamy white bloom. The nectaries are green. The style is thick, smooth and divided into three lobes; the seed pods are smooth and without wings.

It is the disproportionately large blooms on modest stems that are the notable feature of this plant, the discreet foliage emphasizing them further. It is one of many species highly regarded as show plants, this one blooming later than most of those grown for show. As the bulbs increase so slowly it makes good sense to sow seed. The plants do well in pots if grown in a sharply drained compost, moist in the spring and dryish but not completely so in the summer. It is one of the later-flowering species, opening early to midsummer. In the wild it is now restricted to grassy slopes in the southern French Alps at altitudes around 1,500m (5,000ft).

F. t. moggridgei (Boissier & Reuter). A form similar to the type but with yellow flowers flecked brown, 3cm (1¼ inches) long on short stems of 10cm (4 inches).

Fritillaria tuntasia

(1C) Heldreich & Halacsy: lobed–tri: Greece.
This species is easily obtained but difficult to grow; ironically, it is often confused with *F. obliqua*, a rare kind which is difficult to obtain but easy to grow. *F. tuntasia* has orthodox twin-scale small bulbs with a few bulblets clustering near the roots. The stems are 30–45cm (12–18 inches) and very leafy, the lowest lanceolate, the upper linear, grey-green and twisted. They are mainly clustered in the lowest third of the stem, with a few grassy ones near and in among the flowers. These are like grapes, pendant, dark plum-purple to black with a grey bloom; they are wide at the mouth but incurved at the petal ends rather than recurving. Inside the flowers are somewhat lighter but with black nectaries and dark enough to offer a contrast to the yellow anthers. The style has only a token attempt at three-part division; it is often somewhat twisted along its length.

Whereas with most fritillaries a bulb frame is to be preferred to a pot, this species seems to respond better to the latter. It increases only gradually but is a regular bloomer in late spring to early summer. It seems to need cold, dry winter soils, slightly moister spring ones but then returning to near-dry conditions from late summer onwards. This probably mirrors its existence in the wild, where, though rare, it can be found in scrub at altitudes up to 100m (300ft) in the Grecian islands of the Cyclades.

Fritillaria uva–vulpis

(1D) Rix: e: Turkey, Asia Minor.
This plant has been grown under the wrong name for so many years that there is still confusion over the difference between this species and *F. assyriaca*. *F. uva–vulpis* has a large elongated bulb with numerous rounded stolons or bulblets. The stem is 30–45cm (12–18 inches) with a few leaves that are usually glossy but are sometimes covered with a light grey bloom. They are erect and broadly lanceolate, clasping the stems and arranged alternately along it. The solitary or twin bell flowers, borne in mid-spring, are semi-pendant, looking metallic with a steely cast but beneath a purple-brown with yellow at the recurved petal tips. On the inside the petals are golden-brown with an indistinct nectary, smooth and with no colour change. The style is notably thick and entire, nearly filling the centre. The seed pods are smooth and without wings.

F. uva-vulpis is a non-invasive bulb which will soon increase and seed, naturalizing in a well-drained moist soil. While it is not dramatic it is easy and has a claim to elegance.

F. uva–vulpis increases easily by bulb and by seed and will naturalize itself in moist spots of rich soil. Bulbs in the wild find moist spots at levels up to 1,000–1,800m (3,500–6,000ft) in eastern Turkey, northern Iraq and western Iran.

Fritillaria viridia
(6D) Kellogg: tri: Calif.

This species has only very recently become available to gardeners outside the USA, and is likely to be offered as seed rather than bulbs. More will be known about how it will perform in British gardens in a few years' time as seedlings are brought to maturity and tested. The rounded scaly bulbs produce few or no rice grains; the stems are 20–30cm (8–12 inches) high with sharply tipped grey-green grassy foliage held in whorls along them. The flowers, borne from mid- to late spring, are predominantly green with spatterings of darker green, brown or yellow, sometimes forming stripes. The petals

are widely spaced, widely opened and the flowers are pendulous rather in the manner of *F. affinis*. The nectaries are prominently raised and the long yellow anthers almost disguise the trifid style. The seed pods are flat-topped and without wings. This species is found in San Benito County, California, in grassland subject to summer drought, but its distribution is limited.

Fritillaria walujewii
(1B) Regel: tri: Asia.

This rare plant was collected as seed many years ago and is becoming available from British nurseries, albeit slowly. It is closely related to *F. thunbergii* and is often listed with it as a variety. The twin-scaled bulb produces a stem 25–38cm (10–15 inches) tall, the few leaves being opposite and broad at the base though grass-like further up where they are in whorls and have tendril tips. The 1–5 flowers open mid- to late spring and are short, wide pendant bells, the outer three petals being creamy pink though chequered a deeper shade; the inner set of three being lilac-pink chequered purple. The outsides of the nectaries are green to red; inside they are deep green. The trifid style is a distinctive pink. This species comes from the independent republics formerly part of the USSR bordering Afghanistan and Pakistan and the Tien Shan mountain range. It requires the soil to be moist and warm in summer, cold but frost-free during the winter and then moist and cool in spring.

Fritillaria whittallii
(1C) Baker: tri: SW Turkey.

In 1909 a British nursery catalogue offered this plant at £2 per 1000 bulbs, but today you would be lucky to find a packet of seeds for the same price. The bulbs are small and rounded with a few bulblets at the base. The flower stems are 20–25cm (8–10 inches) tall with thin, grey-green, erect leaves arranged alternately along the stem; the flowers, which appear in late spring, are usually solitary but there may be a pair of bells rather like *F. meleagris* in shape and chequered pattern. Each petal is chequered green, brown or purple-black, and incurving at the tips. The nectary is deep green on the inside; the anthers are yellow and the style short and broken.

In the wild *F. whittallii* is to be found growing in rocky places in south-west Turkey. In cultivation it grows with ease in pots or in the bulb frame and will probably be at home outside in well-drained soil.

GLOSSARY

Anther Part of the stamen holding the pollen, splitting when mature and releasing the pollen; held by the filament that arises close to the base of the flower.

Bract Leaf-like growths often below the calyx or base of peduncle.

Capsule Seed pod.

Filament Slender stem holding the anther, affixed to the anther either towards the base or the centre.

Glaucous Non-shiny, dull, possibly with a plum-like bluish bloom.

Lanceolate Descriptive of leaf or petal form, meaning longer than broad by three or more times, broadest at the base.

Linear Descriptive of leaf or petal form, meaning narrow and at least four times longer than broad.

Nectary Nectar vessel at the base of the inner surface of the petal.

Oblanceolate Descriptive of leaves, meaning the same proportions width to length as lanceolate, with the difference that the wider part is about halfway down the length of the leaf.

Ovary Flower part containing ovules (egg cells).

Ovate Descriptive of leaf or petal form, meaning only about twice as long as broad, wider towards the base.

Pedicle Leaf stalk.

Peduncle Flower stalk.

Perianth Sepals and petals (perianth segments) forming the showy part of a flower.

Petals Botanically, the three inner perianth segments; in this book the term is used for both true petals and sepals.

Raceme Descriptive of arrangement of flowers, these being each on equal length stems (peduncles) and evenly distributed.

Sepals Three outer perianth segments.

Stamen Anther and its filament.

Stigma Top area of the style on which pollen can germinate and grow down towards the ovary.

Style Tube from the stigma to the ovary.

Tepals Six perianth segments to include petals and sepals.

Tessellation Chequered patterning.

Tunic Protective tissue wrapped around the bulb as in tulips, less important in fritillaries; it is derived from the degrading of previous season's scales.

Versatile Descriptive of the anthers' deployment, meaning that they are able to swing freely.

Whorled Descriptive of the arrangement of leaves or petals, positioned like spokes of a wheel.

WHERE TO SEE FRITILLARIES

APPENDIX A

There are two main places to see fritillaries – shows and collections. Spring shows, especially those organized by the Alpine Garden Society and in Scotland by the Scottish Rock Garden Club, are likely to have some fritillaries, probably growing in pots. Members of the AGS receive an annual booklet giving full details of shows throughout the coming year; the Nottingham spring show of the AGS is usually particularly strong in fritillaries. Write to the Alpine Garden Society Centre, Avon Bank, Pershore, Worcestershire, WR10 3JP, or to the Scottish Rock Garden Club, Brian Ingham, Sandwood Cottage, Greenbank, Eggleston, Barnards Castle, Co. Durham DL12 0BQ.

The National Council for the Conservation of Plants and Gardens, based at the Royal Horticultural Society Gardens at Wisley in Surrey, was set up to protect gardens and plants that might otherwise be lost forever. It is possibly one of the most underrated of horticultural organizations, doing an enormous amount of work on a voluntary basis; most important are research, identification and understanding of cultivation. There are three NCCPG fritillary collections. A superb representative collection of European species is held at the Cambridge Botanic Gardens, Cory Lodge, Bateman Street, Cambridge, tel. 01223 336265; a collection of *F. imperialis* forms is held by J. Roebuck, the Parks and Recreational Manager at Mandela House, 4 Regent Street, Cambridge, tel. 01223 58977; and the most recently established collection, representing the worldwide distribution of the genus and containing 100 species, is held by Kevin Pratt at Cycad House, 99 Ingleton Road, Edgeley, Stockport SK3 9NR, tel. 0161 4800930.

All National Collections are open to the public. Some have only limited access, but the owners are always willing to help anyone interested in the cultivation of their specialist genus or group of plants. A letter or telephone call to the relevant collection holder will provide you with opening times but, better still, you can buy a National Plant Collections Directory that lists details of all collections. This is available from NCCPG, The Pines, RHS Gardens, Wisley, Woking, Surrey, GU23 6QB, tel. 01483 211465.

Appendix B gives a list of nurseries growing fritillaries. It is worth a telephone call to check whether your planned arrival time is convenient and when there is likely to be the greatest number of flowers to see.

Apart from the Cambridge Botanic Garden other botanic gardens are likely to have some species, for example those at the Royal Botanic Gardens, Kew Road, Richmond, Surrey, tel. 0181 940 1171, and the Royal Botanic Gardens, Inverleith Row, Edinburgh, tel. 01315 527171.

WHERE TO BUY FRITILLARIES

APPENDIX B

BULBS

Jacques Amand Ltd, The Nurseries, Clamp Hill,
Stanmore, Middx HA7 3JS. Tel. 0181 954 8138.

Avon Bulbs, Burnt House Farm, Mid-Lambrook,
South Petherton, Somerset TA13 5HE.
Tel. 01460 242177.

Rupert Bowlby, Gatton, Reigate, Surrey RH2 0TA.
Tel. 01737 642221

Broadleigh Gardens, Barr House, Bishop's Hull,
Taunton, Somerset TA4 2LS. Tel. 01823 286231.

Cambridge Bulbs, Norman Stevens, 40 Whittlesford
Road, Newton, Cambridge CB2 5PH.

Hoog & Dix Export, Heemsteedse Dreef 175, 2101,
KD, Heemstede, Holland.

Martley Bulb & Alpine Nursery, John Hill,
The Laurels, Martley, Worcs WR6 6QA.
Tel. 01886 888762.

Potterton and Martin, The Cottage Nursery,
Moortown Road, Nettleton, Caistor, Lincs LN7
6HX. Tel. 01472 851792.

Janis Ruksaana, LV-4150 Rozula, Cesu Apt, Latvia.

Van Tubergen, Bressingham, Diss, Norfolk IP22 2AB.
Tel. 01379 888282.

Walkers Bulbs, Washway House Farm, Holbeach.
Spalding, Lincs PE12 7PP. Tel. 01406 426216.

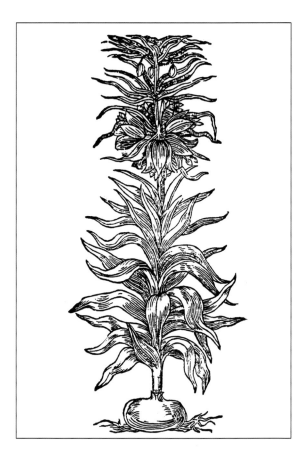

'Corona Imperialis II polyanthus' from Tabernaemontanus's
Eicones plantarum, 1590. This shows a form of *F. imperialis*
with more than one ring of flowers, such as *F. i.* 'Prolifera'
('Crown-on-Crown').

SEEDS

Jim & Jenny Archibald, Bryn Collen, Ffostrasol,
Llandysul, Dyfed SA44 5SB.

Alpine Garden Society, Avon Bank, Pershore,
Worcestershire WR10 3JP. Tel. 01386 554790.
(Members' seed list.)

Chiltern Seeds, Bortree Stile, Ulverston, Cumbria
LA12 7PB. Tel. 01229 581137.

Monocot Nursery, M. R. Salmon, Jacklands,
Jacklands Bridge, Tickenham, Clevedon, Avon
BS21 6SG.

North American Rock Garden Society, Jacques
Mommens, PO Box 67, Millwood, New York 10546,
USA. (Members' seed list.)

Royal Horticultural Society, Lily Group, Dr I. Boyd,
14 Marshalls Way, Wheathampstead, St Albans,
Hertfordshire AL4 8HY (Lily group members'
seed list).

Royal Horticultural Society, Wisley, Woking, Surrey
GU23 6QB. Tel. 01483 224234. (Members' seed
list).

Scottish Rock Garden Club, Brian Ingham, Sandwood
Cottage, Greenbank, Eggleston, Barnard Castle,
Co. Durham DL12 0BQ. (Members' seed list.)

Note:

Information on North American plant sources may be
found in the current edition of the following books:

*The Andersen Horticultural Library's Source List of
Plants and Seeds*. Chanhassen: Minnesota
Landscape Arboretum.

Gardening by Mail and *Taylor's Guide to Specialty
Nurseries*. Barbara J. Barton. New York: Houghton
Mifflin.

'Lilio-Narcissus variegatus atropurpureus Xanctonius'.
From Lobel's *Plantarum seu stripium icones*, 1581. Woodcut
showing a form of *F. meleagris*.

LIST OF SYNONYMS

APPENDIX C

The following are the more commonly encountered synonyms. Note that the same synonym may be used for more than one species.

SYNONYM		SYNONYM	
F. adamantina	F. recurva	F. delphinhensis	F. tubiformis
F. aintabensis	F. imperialis	F. discolor	F. sewerzowii
F. algeriensis	F. messanensis	F. eastwoodiae	F. phaeanthera
F. alpina	F. pinardii	F. eggeri	F. persica
F. altaica	F. thunbergii	F. erzurumica	F. alburyana
F. aquitanica	F. pyrenaica	F. esculenta	F. latifolia
F. arabica	F. persica	F. exima	F. affinis
F. argolica	F. rhodokanakis	F. fleischeri	F. fleischeriana
F. askhabadensis	F. raddeana		F. pinardii
F. askabensis	F. raddeana	F. floribunda	F. affinis
F. assyrica (hort)	F. uva-vulpis	F. foliosa	F. crassifolia kurdica
F. aurea	F. latifolia	F. glaucoviridis	F. alfredae glaucoviridis
F. biebersteiniana	F. latifolia	F. gracilis	F. messanensis gracilis
F. boissieri	F. lusitanica	F. gracillima	F. atropurpurea
F. bonmaensis	F. delavayi	F. graminifolia	F. meleagris
F. bornmulleri	F. latifolia	F. grayana	F. biflora
F. brevicaulis	F. armena	F. grossheimiana	F. crassifolia kurdica
F. burnetii	F. tubiformis	F. guicciardii	F. graeca
F. canasulata	F. assyriaca	F. guilelmi-waldemarii	F. cirrhosa
F. carduchorum	F. minuta	F. gussichiae	F. graeca gussichiae
F. carica	F. bithynica carica	F. heterophylla	F. montana ruthenica
F. caucasica	F. armena caucasica	F. hispanica	F. lusitanica
F. caussolesis	F. montana	F. hutchinsonii	F. brandegeei
F. citrina	F. bithynica		F. messanensis
F. coccinea	F. recurva	F. illyrica	F. messanensis gracilis
F. collina	F. latifolia collina	F. imperialis chitralensis	F. chitralensis
F. collincola	F. thunbergii	F. imperialis eduardii	F. eduardii
F. contorta	F. meleagris contorta	F. ineziana	F. biflora
F. dasyphylla	F. bithynica	F. inflexa	F. biflora

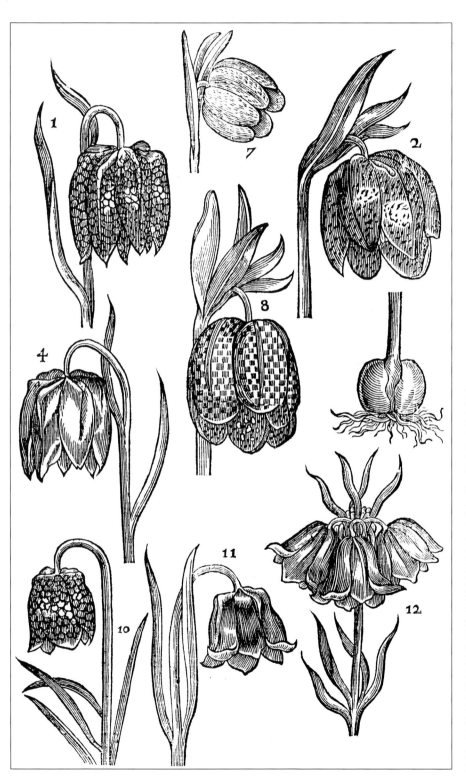

Fritillaries shown in John Parkinson's *Paradisi in sole Paradisus terrestris*, 1629. '1 Fritillaria vulgaris, The common Fritillaria' is *F. meleagris*; '2 Fritillaria flore atrorubens' is a dark form of the same species while '4 Fritillaria alba. The white Fritillaria' is the albino form; '7 Fritillaria lutea puncata' is surely *F. pallidiflora*; '8 Fritillaria lutea Italica' is probably *F. messanensis* despite the yellow suggestion of 'lutea'; '10 F. lutea lusitanica. The small yellow Fritillaria of Portugal' must be *F. lusitanica* while '11 Fritillaria Pyrenea. The black Fritillaria' will be *F. pyrenaica* and '12 Fritillaria umbellifera. The Spanish blacke Fritillaria' is presumably *F. imperialis*.

SYNONYM		SYNONYM	
F. intermis	F. acmopetala	F. orientalis	F. tenella
F. ionica	F. graeca thessala	F. orsiniana	F. montana
F. karadaghensis	F. crassifolia kurdica	F. parviflora	F. micrantha
F. lanceolata	F. affinis	F. persica minor	F. persica
F. leucantha	F. thunbergii	F. pineticola	F. bithynica
F. libanotica	F. persica	F. pinetorum	F. atropurpurea
F. lunellii	F. affinis		pinetorum
F. lurida	F. pyrenaica	F. pontica ionica	F. graeca thessala
F. lutea	F. collina	F. pyrenaica lutescens	F. pyrenaica lutea
	F. latifolia	F. racemosa	F. montana
	F. biebersteiniana	F. roderickii	F. biflora grayana
	F. camschatcensis	F. roylei	F. cirrhosa roylei
	F. lutea	F. rubra	F. armena caucasica
	F. pyrenaica lutea	F. ruthenica	F. montana ruthenica
F. lycia	F. acmopetala	F. schliemannii	F. bithynica
F. longifolia	F. montana meleagroides	F. sieheana	F. elwesii
F. macrandra	F. rhodokanakis	F. skorpilii	F. graeca gussichiae
F. maria	F. lusitanica	F. sphaciottica	F. messanensis
F. mauritanica	F. messanensis	F. stenophylla	F. lusitanica
F. meleagroides	F. montana meleagroides	F. succulenta	F. biflora
F. minor	F. montana ruthenica	F. syriaca	F. pinardii
F. moggridgei	F. tubiformis moggridgei	F. tenella	F. montana
F. multiflora	F. micrantha	F. thessalica	F. graeca thessala
	F. camschatcenis	F. tristis	F. obliqua
F. munbyi	F. messanensis	F. tulipifera	F. armena
F. mutica	F. affinis	F. umbellata	F. pyrenaica
F. neglecta	F. messanensis gracilis	F. unicolor	F. graeca
	F. montana	F. urmensis	F. graeca
F. nervosa	F. pyrenaica	F. verticillata	F. thunbergii
	F. nigra	F. viridiflora	F. bithynica viridiflora
	F. montana	F. walujewii	F. thunbergii walujewii
F. nigra	F. montana	F. wanensis	F. crassifolia kurdica
F. nobilis	F. latifolia	F. zagrica	F. armena zagrica
F. ochridiana	F. graeca	F. zahnii	F. graeca
F. ojaiensis	F. affinis	Guilelmi waldemarii	F. cirrhosa
F. olympica	F. pontica	Korolkowia sewerzowii	F. sewerzowii
F. ophioglosifolia	F. crassifolia	Petilium chitralensis	F. chitralensis
F. oranensis	F. messanensis atlantica	Petilium eduardii	F. eduardii

FRITILLARIES FOR SPECIFIC LOCATIONS

APPENDIX D

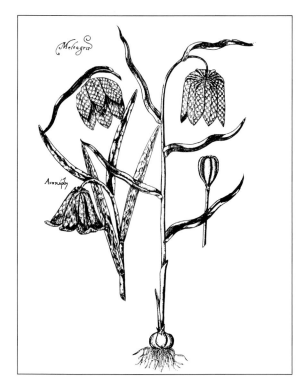

F. meleagris from Paul Renealme's *Specimen historiae plantarum*, 1611. An attractive illustration showing flower, leaves, corm, and seed capsule very accurately.

FRITILLARIES FOR OPEN GROUND

F. acmopetala

F. affinis

F. biflora 'Martha Roderick'

F. imperialis

F. meleagris

F. michailovskyi

F. pallidiflora

F. persica

F. pontica

F. pyrenaica

FRITILLARIES FOR SUNNY PLACES

F. acmopetala

F. biflora 'Martha Roderick'

F. imperialis

F. latifolia

F. libanotica

F. meleagris

F. messanensis

F. messanensis gracilis

F. michailovskyi

F. persica

F. pyrenaica

F. raddeana

FRITILLARIES FOR SHADE

F. affinis

F. camschatcensis

F. graeca thessala

F. imperialis

F. involucrata

F. obliqua

F. pallidiflora

F. persica (partial shade)

F. pontica

F. thunbergii

F. tuntasia

FRITILLARIES FOR MORAINE
(i.e scree with water beneath)

F. acmopetala

F. latifolia

F. pontica

F. pudica

F. pyrenaica

FRITILLARIES PARTICULARLY SUITED TO POT CULTURE

F. agrestis

F. alfredae

F. alfredae glaucoviridis

F. armena

F. armena caucasica

F. atropurpurea

F. biflora

F. bithynica

F. bithynica viridiflora

F. conica

F. crassifolia

F. crassifolia kurdica

F. drenovskyi

F. ehrhartii

F. falcata

F. glauca

F. graeca

F. latifolia

F. liliacea

F. lusitanica

F. messanensis

F. messanensis gracilis

'Lilium persicum' from *Hortus floridus* of Crispin de Pas, 1614. An accurate and pleasing representation of *F. persica* with visiting butterfly.

F. michailovskyi

F. montana

F. montana meleagroides

F. montana ruthenica

F. olivieri

F. oranensis

F. pluriflora

F. pudica

F. purdyi

F. recurva

F. rhodokansis

F. sibthorpiana

F. tubiformis

F. tubiformis moggridgei

FRITILLARIES FOR ROCK GARDENS

F. agrestis

F. biflora

F. biflora 'Martha Roderick'

F. davisii

F. drenovskyi

F. ehrhartii

F. glauca

F. graeca

F. graeca thessala

F. lusitanica

F. meleagris

F. meleagroides

F. messanensis

F. pontica

F. pudica

F. pyrenaica

F. tubiformis

F. uva vulpis

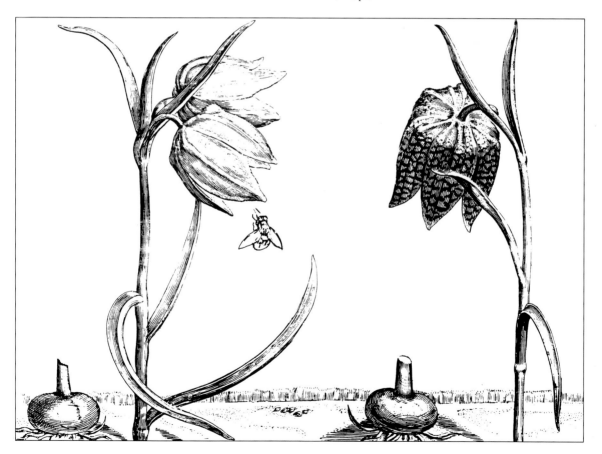

'Frittillaria flore albo' and 'Frittillaria flore purpureo' from *Hortus floridus* of Crispin de Pas, 1614. Very attractive representations of forms of *F. meleagris*, giving good three-dimensional effect.

COUNTRY OF ORIGIN

APPENDIX E

EUROPEAN FRITILLARIES

F. caucasica

F. conica

F. davisii

F. drenovskyi

F. ehrhartii

F. graeca

F. graeca thessala

F. involucrata

F. latifolia

F. macrantha

F. meleagris

F. messanensis

F. montana

F. nobilis

F. obliqua

F. oranensis

F. pontica

F. pyrenaica

F. rhodokanensis

F. montana ruthenica

F. sibthorpiana

F. stribrnyi

F. tubiformis

F. tuntasia

EASTERN MEDITERRANEAN & ASIA MINOR FRITILLARIES

F. acmopetala

F. alfredae glaucoviridis

F. armena

F. aurea

F. bithynica

F. crassifolia

F. crassifolia kurdica

F. dasyphylla

F. elwesii

F. libanotica

F. montana

F. montana meleagroides

'Lilium sive Corona Imperialis', from Lobel's *Plantarum seu stripium icones*, 1581, showing *F. imperialis* in flower and fruit (right).

F. *montana ruthenica*

F. *persica*

F. *whitallii*

ASIAN FRITILLARIES

F. *assyriaca*

F. *bucharica*

F. *camschatcensis*

F. *cirrhosa*

F. *cirrhosa roylei*

F. *fusca*

F. *imperialis*

F. *japonica*

F. *karelinii*

F. *olivieri*

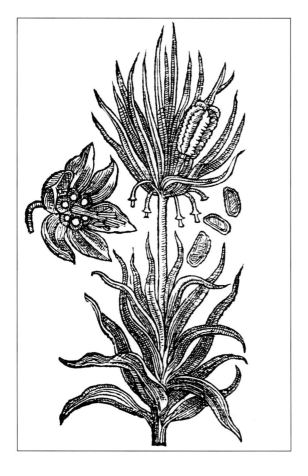

F. *pallidiflora*

F. *persica*

F. *raddeana*

F. *sewerzowii*

F. *thunbergii*

F. *zagrica*

NORTH AMERICAN FRITILLARIES

F. *affinis*	California
F. *agrestis*	California
F. *atropurpurea*	Arizona, California, Colorado, N. Dakota, S. Dakota, Idaho, Montana, Nebraska, Nevada, Oregon, Utah, Wyoming
F. *biflora*	California
F. *brandegeei*	California
F. *camschatcensis*	Alaska, British Columbia, Washington
F. *falcata*	California
F. *glauca*	California, Oregon
F. *lanceolata*	British Columbia, California, Idaho, Oregon, Washington
F. *liliacea*	California
F. *micrantha*	California
F. *phaeanthera*	California
F. *pluriflora*	California, Oregon
F. *pudica*	Alberta, British Columbia, Idaho, Montana, Nevada, Oregon, Utah, Washington, Wyoming
F. *purdyi*	California
F. *recurva*	California, Nevada, Oregon
F. *striata*	California

PLANT CHARACTERISTICS & REQUIREMENTS

APPENDIX F

SPECIES	FLOWERING PERIOD	SIZE
acmopetala	mid- to late spring	30–50cm (12–20in)
acmopetala wendelboi	late spring	10cm (4in)
affinis	late spring to early summer	20cm (8in)
affinis tristulis	late spring	20cm (8in)
affinis 'Limelight'	late spring	40–60cm (16–24in)
affinis 'Wayne Roderick'	late spring	20cm (8in)
agrestis	mid-spring to early summer	30–40cm (12–16in)
alburyana	late spring to midsummer	5–10cm (2–4in)
alfredae	mid-spring	15–30cm (6–12in)
ariana	late spring to early summer	25cm (10in)
armena	early to mid-spring	4–7.5cm (1½–2in)
armena caucasica	early to mid-spring	15–20cm (6–8in)
assyriaca	mid-spring	20–25cm (8–10in)
atropurpurea	mid-spring to early summer	40–60cm (16–24in)
biflora	late winter to late spring	25–40cm (10–16in)
biflora grayana	mid-spring to early summer	10–20cm (4–8in)
biflora 'Martha Roderick'	early summer	20cm (8in)
bithynica	mid- to late spring	10–15cm (4–6in)
carica	early to late spring	10–15cm (4–6in)
brandegeei	midsummer	60cm (24in)
bucharica	mid- to late spring	20–30cm (8–12in)
camschatcensis	midsummer	20–40cm (8–16in)
camschatcensis lutea	midsummer	30cm (12in)
chitralensis	mid- to late spring	10cm (4in)
chlorantha	late spring	5–10cm (2–4in)
cirrhosa	late spring to early summer	15–30cm (6–12in)
conica	mid- to late spring	13–20cm (5–8in)
crassifolia	late spring to early summer	15–25cm (6–10in)

COLOUR	EASY OR DIFFICULT	SUMMER SOIL
green and purple	easy	well-drained loam
green and purple	easy	well-drained loam
purple and green	easy	dry, clay
purple	easy	dry
green	easy	dry
creamy brown and black	easy	dry
white or lime yellow	difficult	dry
pink	alpine house, difficult	dry
green	alpine house, easy	dry
pink	alpine house, difficult	moist peat
purple or green	easy	dry
brown	easy	dry
purple to brown	easy	dry/leafy
reddish brown	moderate	dry
green and brown/black	easy	dry
reddish brown and white	easy	dry
brown and white	easy	dry
yellow to green	easy	dry
yellow	easy	dry
muddy white stars	difficult	dry
creamy green	difficult	dry
plum purple	easy	wet peat
yellow-green	easy	wet peat
gold to yellow	moderate	dry
green	difficult	dry
green and brown	moderate	dry
yellow	alpine house, moderate	dry
green or brown-green	moderate	dry

SPECIES	FLOWERING PERIOD	SIZE
crassifolia kurdica	late winter to early spring	10–20cm (4–8in)
crassifolia hakkarensis	early to mid-spring	5cm (2in)
davisii	late spring to early summer	7.5–15cm (3–6in)
delavayi	midsummer	5cm (2in)
drenovskyi	early to mid-spring	20–25cm (8–10in)
eduardii	mid- to late spring	60–76cm (24–30in)
ehrhartii	early spring	10–15cm (4–6in)
elwesii	mid- to late spring	25–40cm (10–16in)
epirotica	early summer	7.5–10cm (3–4in)
euboeica	late spring	7.5–10cm (3–4in)
falcata	late spring to early summer	2–7.5cm (1–3in)
fleischeriana	late spring	7.5cm (3in)
forbesii	early to mid-spring	15–20cm (6–8in)
gibbosa	late spring to early summer	7.5–20cm (3–8in)
glauca	late spring to early summer	10–13cm (3–4in)
graeca	early spring to midsummer	35cm (14in)
graeca thessala	mid- to late spring	20–30cm (8–12in)
gussichae	mid-spring	25–38cm (10–15in)
hermonis amana	mid- to late spring	13–17cm (5–7in)
hermonis amana 'E. K. Balls'	mid- to late spring	10cm (4in)
hermonis amana lutea	mid- to late spring	13–15cm (5–6in)
imperialis lutea	early to midsummer	90cm (36in)
imperialis 'Lutea Maxima'	early to midsummer	120cm (48in)
imperialis 'Rubra'	early to midsummer	90cm (36in)
imperialis 'Rubra Maxima'	early to midsummer	120cm (48in)
imperialis aurora	early to midsummer	60cm (24in)
imperialis 'The Premier'	early to midsummer	60cm (24in)
imperialis 'Sulpherino'	early to midsummer	90cm (36in)
imperialis 'Prolifera'	early to midsummer	60cm (24in)
imperialis 'Aureomarginata'	early to midsummer	90cm (36in)
involucrata	late spring	25–35cm (10–14in)
kotschyana	early spring	15cm (6in)
latakiensis	late spring to early summer	25–40cm (10–16in)
latifolia	mid- to late spring	15cm (6in)

COLOUR	EASY OR DIFFICULT	SUMMER SOIL
brown, red and yellow	easy	dry
green	alpine house, difficult	dry
glossy brown	easy	dry
grey to brown	alpine house, difficult	gritty, dry
purple	difficult	moist
orange	easy	dry
purple	difficult	cool peat
green and black	easy	dry
brown	difficult	dry
yellow	alpine house, difficult	dry
multicoloured	alpine house, difficult	dry
purple	alpine house, moderate	dry
yellow	alpine house, easy	dry
pink	alpine house, moderate	dry
yellow	alpine house, moderate	dry clay
red and green	easy	moist
red and brown	moderate	dry
yellow to green	alpine house, difficult	dry humus
green	easy	dry
brown and green	easy	dry
yellow	alpine house, easy	dry
yellow	easy	dry
yellow	easy	dry
red	easy	dry
red	easy	dry
orange	easy	dry
red	easy	dry
orange and purple	easy	dry
orange and purple	easy	dry
variegated foliage	easy	dry
creamy green	easy	dry
red	alpine house, easy	dry
purple	easy	dry
red	moderate	dry

SPECIES	FLOWERING PERIOD	SIZE
latifolia aurea	mid- to late spring	2.5–13cm (1–5in)
liliacea	late spring to early summer	15–30cm (6–12in)
lusitanica	mid- to late spring	20–30cm (8–12in)
meleagris	mid- to late spring	20–38cm (8–15in)
meleagris 'Aphrodite'	mid- to late spring	20–38cm (8–15in)
meleagris 'Artemis'	mid- to late spring	30–38cm (12–15in)
meleagris 'Charon'	mid- to late spring	20–25cm (8–10in)
meleagris 'Jupiter'	mid- to late spring	20–25cm (8–10in)
meleagris 'Orion'	mid- to late spring	20–25cm (8–10in)
meleagris 'Pink Eveline'	mid- to late spring	38–50cm (15–20in)
meleagris 'Poseidon'	mid- to late spring	20–25cm (8–10in)
meleagris 'Saturnus'	mid- to late spring	20–25cm (8–10in)
messanensis	late spring	30–40cm (12–16in)
messanensis gracilis	late spring	15–20cm (6–8in)
michailovskyi	late spring to early summer	10–15cm (4–6in)
micrantha	late spring	20–25cm (8–10in)
minima	mid- to late spring	5cm (2in)
minuta	mid- to late spring	10–15cm (4–6in)
montana	mid-spring to early summer	25cm (10in)
montana ruthenica	late spring to early summer	25–30cm (10–20in)
obliqua	late spring	15–20cm (6–8in)
oliveri	mid- to late spring	30–38cm (12–15in)
pallidiflora	early summer	20–45cm (8–18in)
persica	early to midsummer	100cm (40in)
persica 'Adiyaman'	early to midsummer	60cm (24in)
phaeanthera	mid- to late spring	30cm (12in)
pinardii	mid- to late spring	5–10cm (2–4in)
pluriflora	late spring to early summer	23–30cm (9–12in)
pontica	late spring to early summer	20–38cm (8–15in)
pudica	late spring to early summer	7.5–13cm (3–5in)
purdyi	mid- to late spring	13–18cm (5–7in)
pyrenaica	late spring to early summer	25–45cm (10–18in)
pyrenaica lutea	late spring to early summer	25–45cm (10–18in)
raddeana	mid- to late spring	50–76cm (20–30in)

COLOUR	EASY OR DIFFICULT	SUMMER SOIL
yellow	alpine house, moderate	dry
white	alpine house, moderate	dry
red and brown	easy	moist
reds and purples	easy	moist
white	easy	moist
red and grey	easy	moist
purple	easy	moist
red	easy	moist
violet	easy	moist
pink	easy	moist
purple to pink	easy	moist
blood red	easy	moist
brown and red	moderate	dry
brown red	moderate	dry
yellow and brown	easy	dry
mauve brown	alpine house, difficult	dry clay
yellow	alpine house, difficult	dry
brown	easy	cool dry
purple and brown	easy	dry
red and yellow	easy	dry
black	easy	dry
brown and green	easy	dry
primrose yellow	easy	dry
plum purple	easy	dry
plum purple	easy	dry
orange and yellow	alpine house, difficult	dry
purple or purple and yellow	moderate	cool, dry
pink	alpine house, difficult	dry clay
green	easy	dry
orange or yellow and gold	easy	dry
multicoloured	alpine house, moderate	dry
gold, green and brown	easy	dry
yellow	easy	dry
primrose yellow	easy	dry

SPECIES	FLOWERING PERIOD	SIZE
recurva	early summer	40–60cm (16–24in)
recurva coccinea	early summer	40–60cm (16–24in)
reuteri	mid-spring	18–25cm (7–10in)
sewerzowii	early to mid-spring	25–40cm (10–16in)
sibthropiana	late spring	10–15cm (4–6in)
stenanthera	early to mid-spring	15–25cm (6–10in)
thunbergii	mid- to late spring	60–76cm (24–30in)
tubiformis	early to mid-spring	10–20cm (4–8in)
tuntasia	late spring to early summer	30–46cm (12–18in)
uva-vulpis	mid-spring	30–46cm (12–18in)
viridia	late spring	20–30cm (8–12in)
walujewii	late spring	25–38cm (10–15in)
whittallii	late spring	20–25cm (8–10in)

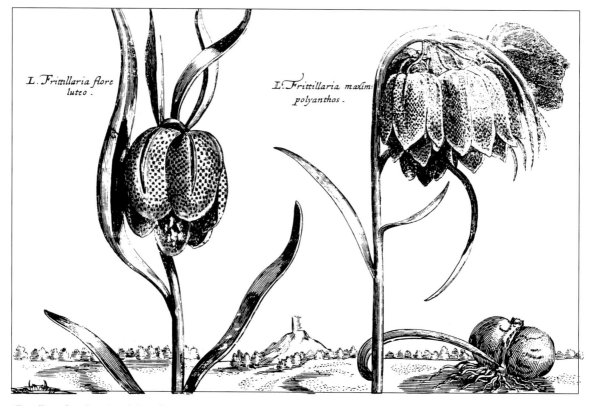

'Frittillaria flore luteo' and 'Frittillaria maxima polyanthos' from *Hortus floridus* of Crispin de Pas, 1614. Although they are beautifully drawn correct identification is difficult; 'F. flore luteo' may be a form of *F. latifolia* such as *F. l. collina* and 'F. maxima polyanthos' could be *F. pontica*.

COLOUR	EASY OR DIFFICULT	SUMMER SOIL
red	alpine house, moderate	dry
yellow and red	alpine house, moderate	dry
red and yellow	alpine house, moderate	cool, moist
green and brown	alpine house, moderate	dry
gold	alpine house, easy	dry
pink to purple	alpine house, moderate	dry
cream and green	easy	moist peat
grey, red and purple	alpine house, easy	dry
black	alpine house, difficult	dry
brown and gold	easy	moist
green	alpine house, difficult	dry
creamy pink	alpine house, moderate	warm and moist
green and brown	difficult	dry

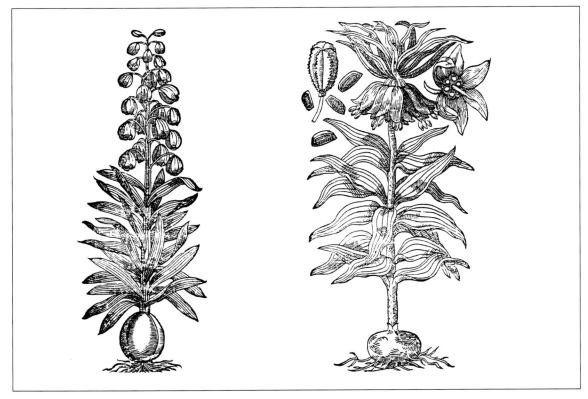

'Lilium persicum' and 'Corona Imperialis' from *Eicones plantarum* by John Theodor (Latinized as Tabernaemontanus) 1590. *Lilium persicum* is *F. persica* and Corona imperialis is *F. imperialis*. Both are remarkably good likenesses for such an early work, the bulbs being well rendered.

INDEX

Page numbers in *italic* refer to illustrations

Acknowledgements

The authors would like to thank all those who have helped us in making this book. We are especially grateful to Kath Dryden, Christopher Grey-Wilson and John Hill who willingly gave their time and expertise to form the chapter People and their Plants. They have added considerably to the value of the book. The unfailing patience and helpfulness of Dr Brent Elliott and his team at the RHS Lindley Library is something all who use this valued facility come to expect; we are deeply grateful for the reliable and good-natured help. We thank Jim Almond and Francis Ferns for the opportunity to photograph flowers when our own were either not out or over. The Alpine Garden Society have a fine picture editor in Mrs Jo Stalland, I thank her for her kind help in searching through the AGS slide library to find suitable pictures of kinds we needed. David & Charles are expert publishers; we thank their staff for their professional help and must say a very big thank you to Anna Mumford who has looked after our work, we thank her for her friendship and patience.